mini atlas

Bartholomew

Edinburgh

1974

© John Bartholomew & Son Ltd., Edinburgh
Printed and Published in Great Britain by
John Bartholomew & Son Ltd. 1974
ISBN 0 85152 315 3
5763

Contents

Contents

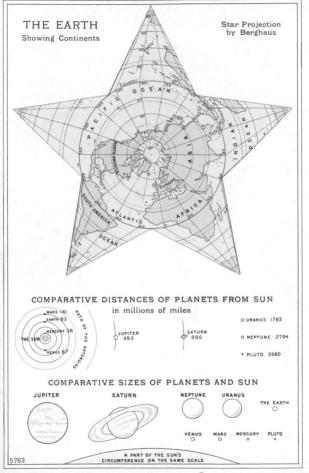

THE EARTH
Showing Continents

Star Projection
by Berghaus

COMPARATIVE DISTANCES OF PLANETS FROM SUN
in millions of miles

MARS 141
EARTH 93
MERCURY 36
THE SUN
VENUS 67
PATH OF THE ASTEROIDS

JUPITER
483

SATURN
886

○ URANUS 1783

○ NEPTUNE 2794

• PLUTO 3560

COMPARATIVE SIZES OF PLANETS AND SUN

JUPITER   SATURN   NEPTUNE   URANUS   THE EARTH

VENUS   MARS   MERCURY   PLUTO

A PART OF THE SUN'S
CIRCUMFERENCE ON THE SAME SCALE

5763

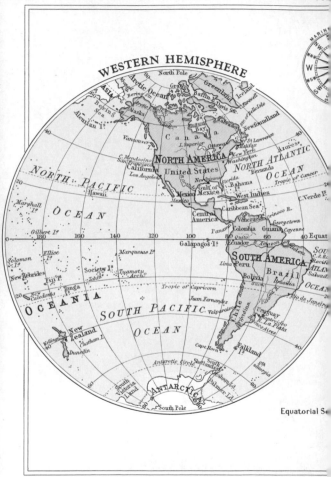

WESTERN HEMISPHERE

North Pole

ARCTIC Ocean

Greenland

Iceland

ASIA

Baffin Bay

Davis Str.

Bering Sea

Arctic Cir.

C. Farewell

Alaska

Aleutian Is.

Labrador

Str. of Belle Isle

Newfoundland

Vancouver

Hudson Bay

St. Lawrence

C a n a d a

L. Superior

Ottawa

Halifax

NORTH ATLANTIC

Azores

C. Mendocino

San Francisco

California

New York

Washington

Bermuda

OCEAN

Los Angeles

NORTH AMERICA

United States

Tropic of Cancer

NORTH PACIFIC

Hawaii

New Orleans

Florida

Gulf of

Mexico

Bahama

West Indies

C. Verde Is.

OCEAN

Mexico

Caribbean Sea

Marshall Is.

Central

Venezuela

Orinoco R.

Georgetown

Gilbert Is.

180

160

140

120

100

America

Panama

80

Colombia

60

Guiana

Cayenne

40

Equat.

Quito

Ecuador

Amazon

Galapagos Is.

Marquesas Is.

Lima

Peru

SOUTH AMERICA

C. S. Roque

Recife

ATLANTIC

Solomon

Is.

Ellice

Is.

Society Is.

Tahiti

Tuamotu

Arch.

Brazil

Salvad.

OCEAN

New Hebrides

Fiji Is.

Tonga

Bolivia

Brasilia

New Caledonia

OCEANIA

Tropic of Capricorn

Sucre

Rio de Janeiro

Juan Fernandez

Chile

Montevideo

Uruguay

R. la Plata

SOUTH PACIFIC

Valparaiso

Buenos Aires

New Zealand

Wellington

Chatham I.

OCEAN

Cape Horn

Falkland

Is.

Sth. Georgia

Dunedin

Antarctic Circle

Shetland Is.

South

Palmer Ld.

Victoria Land

ANTARCTICA

Graham Ld.

South Pole

Equatorial S

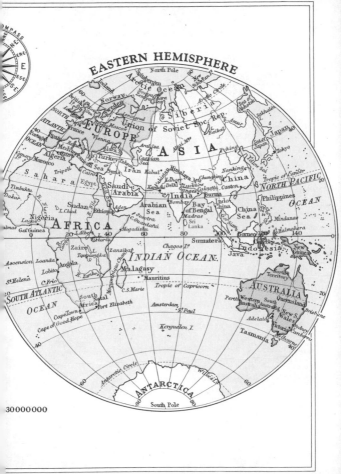

EASTERN HEMISPHERE

30 000 000

© – John Bartholomew & Son, Ltd, Edinburgh.

4

RELIEF

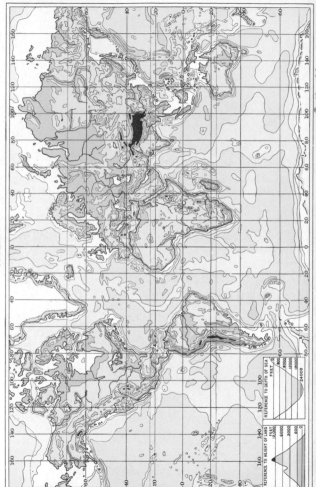

ARCTIC OCEAN

New Siberian Is

Sea of Okhotsk

Bering Sea

Tropic of Cancer

Urals

INDIAN OCEAN

AUSTRALIA

EUROPE

ASIA

S a h a r a

AFRICA

ATLANTIC OCEAN

Greenland

West Indies

NORTH AMERICA

SOUTH AMERICA

PACIFIC OCEAN

Hudson Bay

Baffin Land

Tropic of Capricorn

Galapagos Is

Tristan da Cunha

St Helena

Ascension

Labrador Current

Gulf Stream

Arctic Current

Canaries Current

North Equatorial Current

South Equatorial Current

Guinea Current

Benguela Current

Brazil Current

Falkland Current

West Wind Drift

Vancouver

California Current

West Australian Current

Mozambique Current

Agulhas Current

Tropic of Cancer

Legend

Cold Currents
Warm Currents
Limit of Floating Ice

Tundra and Alpine
Coniferous Forest
Mixed Cultivation and Forest
Tropical Forest
Semi-Arid Cultivation
Desert

© – John Bartholomew & Son Ltd. Edinburgh.

TEMPERATURE—JANUARY

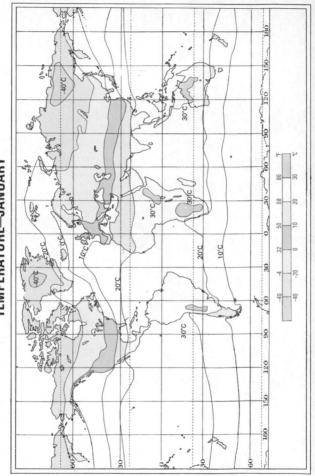

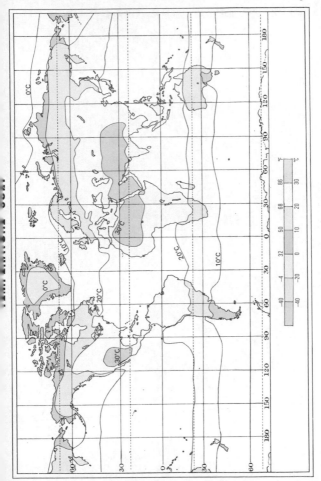

COMMUNICATIONS

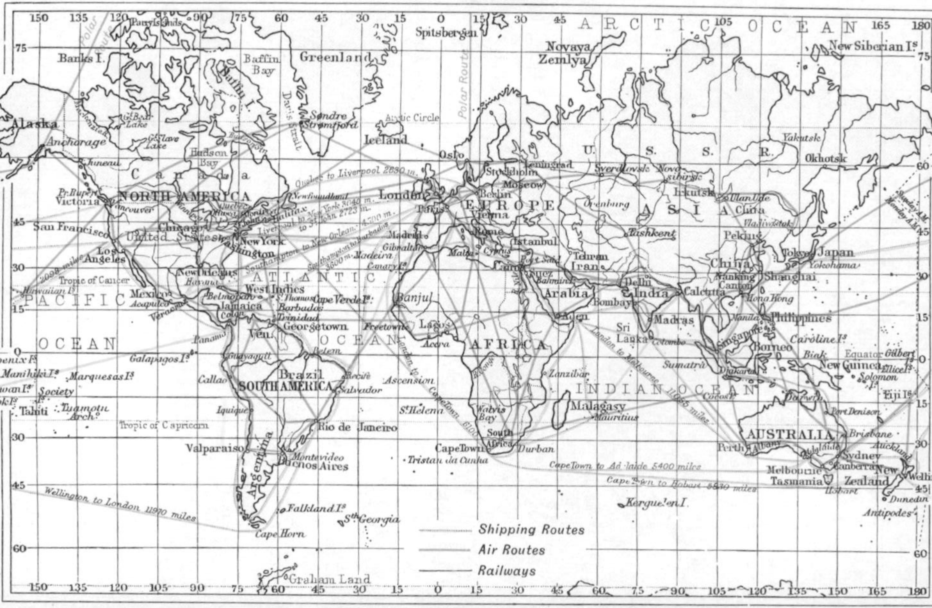

Legend:
- —— Shipping Routes
- —— Air Routes
- —— Railways

9

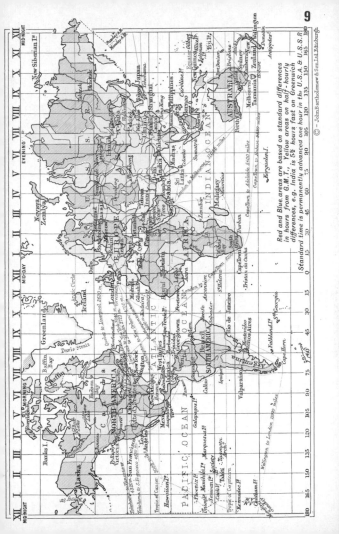

Red and Blue areas are based on standard differences in hours from G.M.T. Yellow areas on half-hourly differences, e.g. India is 5½ hours fast on Greenwich Standard time is permanently advanced one hour in the U.S.A. & U.S.S.R.

© John Bartholomew & Son. Ltd. Edinburgh.

NORTH AMERICA

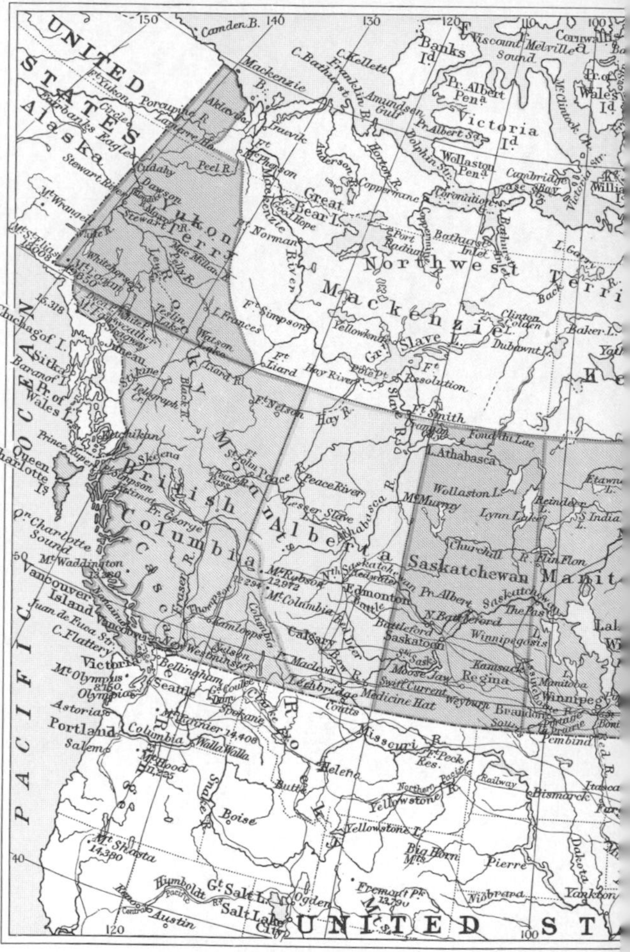
UNITED STATES
Alaska
Yukon Terr.
Northwest Terri
Mackenzie
British Columbia
Alberta
Saskatchewan
Manit
PACIFIC OCEAN
UNITED ST
Banks Id.
Victoria Id.
Viscount Melville Sound
Prince of Wales Id.
Cornwallis
Great Bear L.
Gr. Slave L.
L. Athabasca
Wollaston L.
Reindeer L.
Lynn Lake
Flin Flon
Winnipegosis
Winnipeg
Brandon
Regina
Saskatoon
Moose Jaw
Swift Current
Medicine Hat
Lethbridge
Calgary
Edmonton
Pr. Albert
N. Battleford
Battleford
The Pas
Peace River
Prince Rupert
Kamloops
Vancouver
New Westminster
Victoria
Vancouver Island
Queen Charlotte Is.
Juneau
Sitka
Ketchikan
Skagway
Whitehorse
Dawson
Fairbanks
Circle
Eagle
Aklavik
Inuvik
Ft. McPherson
Ft. Good Hope
Ft. Norman
Ft. Simpson
Ft. Liard
Ft. Nelson
Ft. Resolution
Ft. Smith
Ft. McMurray
Port Radium
Yellowknife
Hay River
Seattle
Portland
Salem
Spokane
Helena
Butte
Boise
Bismarck
Pierre
Yankton
Salt Lake City
Ogden
Austin
Mt. Logan 19,850
Mt. St. Elias 18,008
Mt. Robson 12,972
Mt. Shasta 14,380
Mt. Hood 11,225
Mt. Rainier 14,408
Fremont Pk. 13,790
Mt. Columbia
Missouri R.
Yellowstone R.
Columbia
Snake R.
Mackenzie River
Peace
Athabasca R.
Liard R.
Saskatchewan
150
140
130
120
110
100
50
40

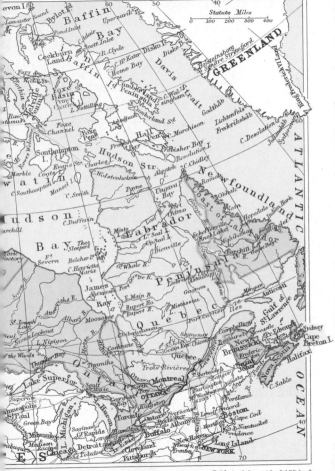

WESTERN PROVINCES

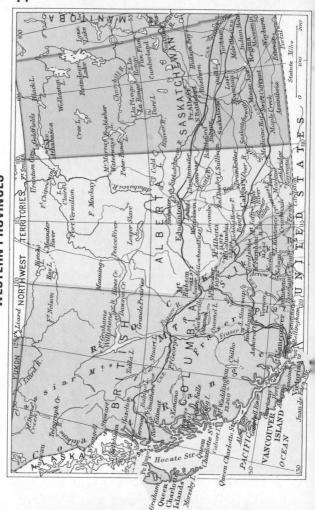

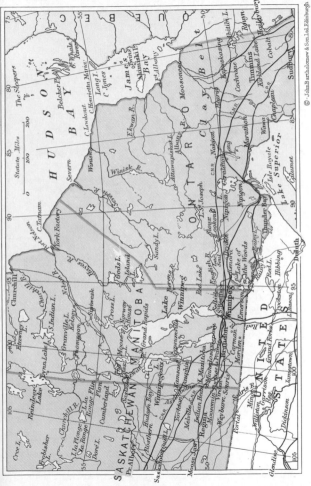

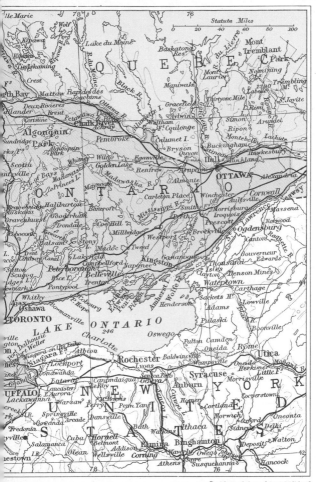

QUEBEC

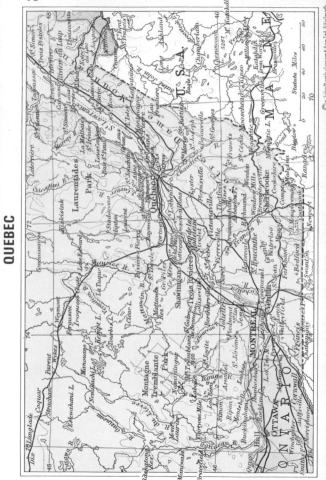

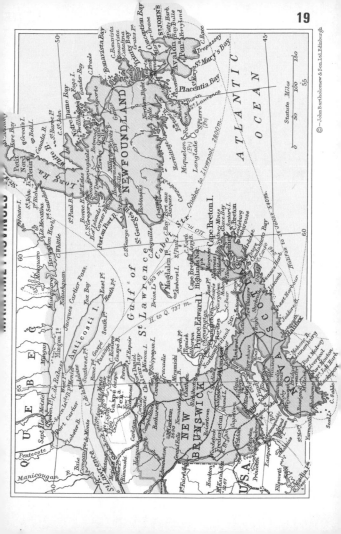

© J.ohn Bartholomew & Son. Ltd. Edinburgh&

ATLANTIC OCEAN

Statute Miles

0   50   100   150
55

NEWFOUNDLAND

ST. JOHN'S
Conception Bay
Trinity Bay
C. Bonavista
C. Freels
Fogo I.
Notre Dame Bay

C. Race
Placentia Bay
St. Mary's Bay
Trepassey
St. Pierre (Fr.)
Miquelon (Fr.)
Fortune Bay
Hermitage Bay

QUEBEC

Gulf of St. Lawrence

Anticosti I.

Cape Breton I.

PRINCE EDWARD I.

NOVA SCOTIA

NEW BRUNSWICK

Fredericton

U.S.A.

C. Sable

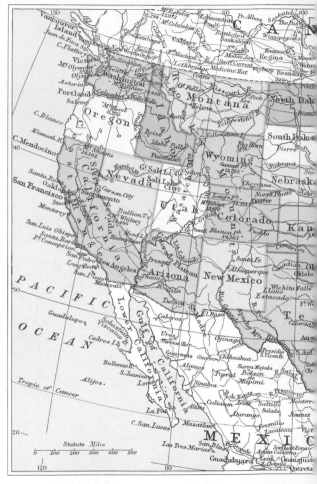

EASTERN STATES

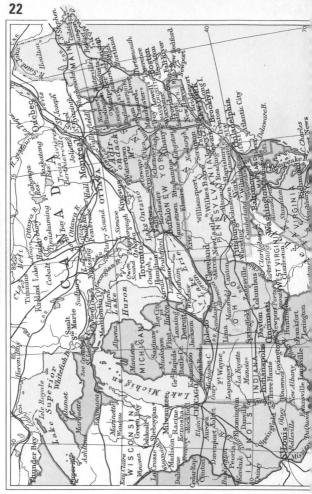

MIDDLE ATLANTIC COAST

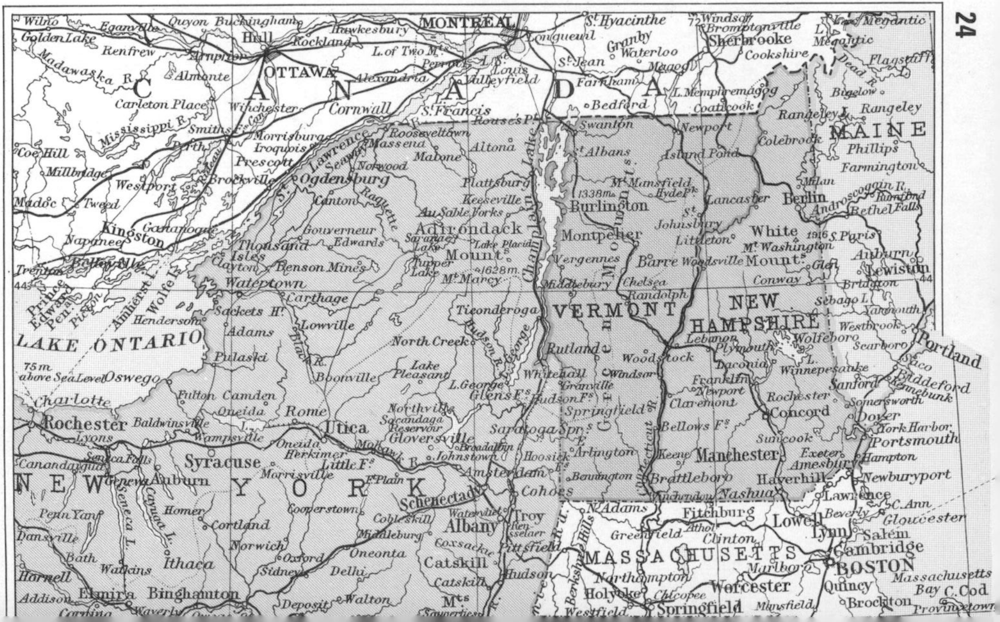

MAINE
NEW HAMPSHIRE
VERMONT
MASSACHUSETTS
NEW YORK
CANADA
MONTREAL
OTTAWA
LAKE ONTARIO

Portland
Boston
Cambridge
Worcester
Springfield
Albany
Schenectady
Troy
Syracuse
Rochester
Utica
Rome
Ithaca
Binghamton
Oneonta
Concord
Manchester
Montpelier
Burlington
Rutland
Kingston

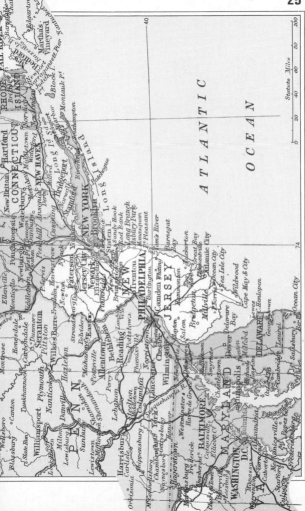

ATLANTIC

OCEAN

Statute Miles

0   20   40   60   80   100

RHODE ISLAND

FALL RIVER

CONNECTICUT

NEW HAVEN

NEW YORK

Long Island

Brooklyn

Jersey City

Newark

Paterson

Staten I.

NEW JERSEY

PHILADELPHIA

Trenton

Camden

Reading

Allentown

Bethlehem

PENN.

Scranton

Wilkes-Barre

Harrisburg

Carlisle

Lancaster

York

Columbia

Wilmington

Chester

DELAWARE

Delaware Bay

Dover

MARYLAND

BALTIMORE

Annapolis

WASHINGTON D.C.

Atlantic City

Cape May & City

Ocean City

Williamsport

Danville

Hazleton

Pottsville

Sunbury

ERIE AND OHIO BASINS

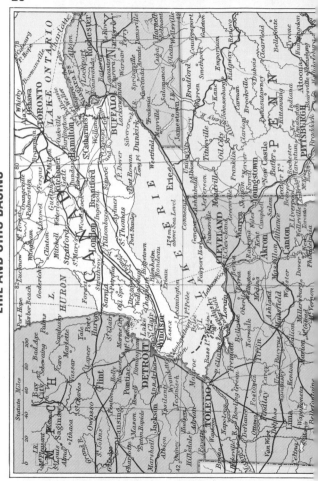

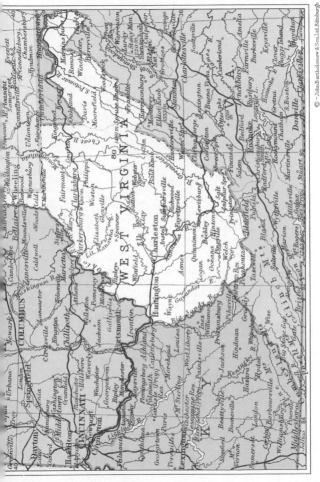

© - John Bartholomew & Son, Ltd, Edinburgh

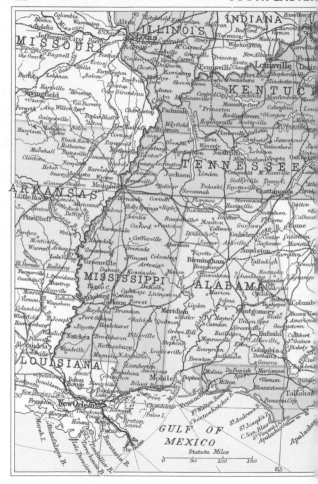

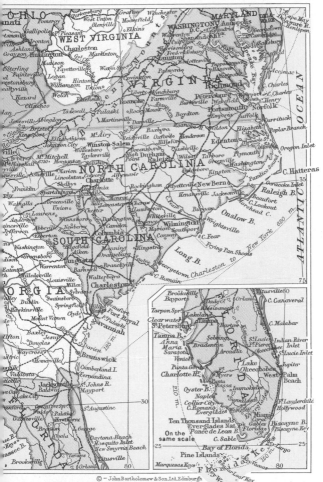

CENTRAL STATES

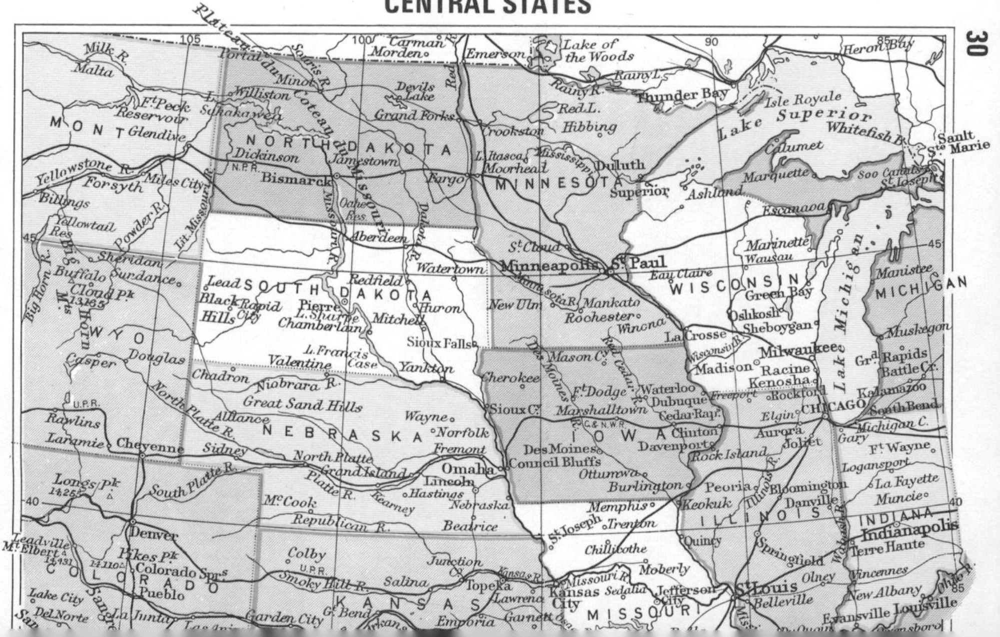

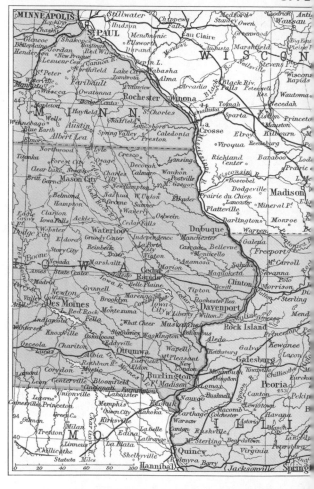

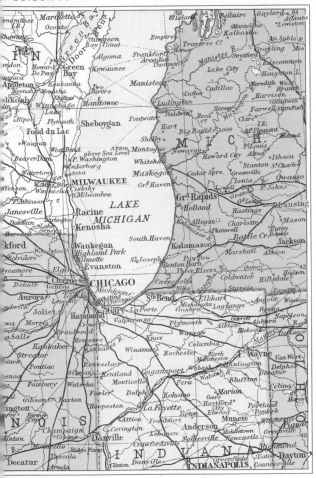

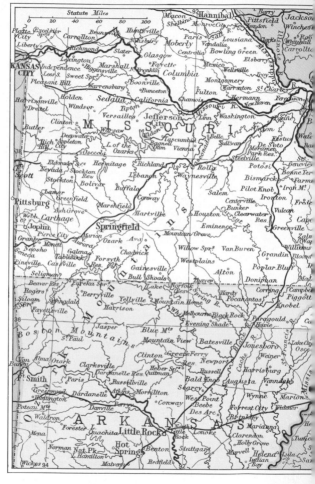

Statute Miles
0 20 40 60 80 100

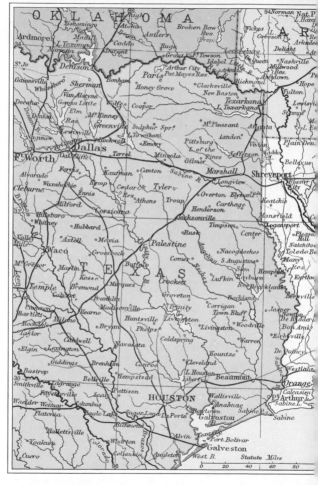

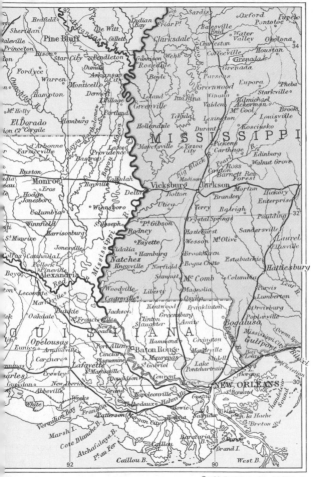

© – John Bartholomew & Son.Ltd.Edinburgh.

38

WESTERN STATES

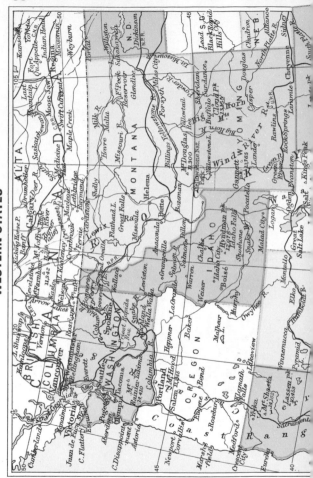

This is a map of the southwestern United States and northern Mexico.

COLORADO
Ikes Pk., Colorado Spr., Pueblo, Leadville, Mt.Elbert 14421, Grand Junction, Montrose, Sangre de Cristo Mts., Blanc.Pk 14363, Trinidad, Las Animas

Rio Pecos, Santa Fe, 35, Farwell, Pecos

NEW MEXICO
Albuquerque, Las Vegas, Lincoln, Roswell, Rio Grande, Socorro, Las Cruces, El Paso, Ciudad Juarez, Mt.Taylor 11389, S.F.R., San Juan Mts., Silverton, Durango, Lake City, Del Norte

UTAH
Bluff, S.Juan R., Carizo Mts 9416, Mt San Francisco 12611, Colorado Plateau, Gila R., San Carlos, Demino, Sierra Madre Plateau, Janos

Salt L., Lake Powell, Mt.Wood Canyon, Hoover Dam, Lt.Mead, St George, Jupiter, Ashfork, Havasu L., Prescott, Phoenix, Tucson, S.P.R., Nogales, Cananea, Altar, Arispe, Moctezuma, Cumpas, Agua Prieta, Hermosillo, R. Sonora, Tres, R. Yaqui

ARIZONA
Colorado R., Yuma, Topolobampo

MEXICO
Chihuahua, Galeana, Martia, Presidio, Condp., Guerrero

Carson City, Walker L., Tonopah, Pioche, Wheeler Pk., Belmont 13063, Delano Pk., Zion

NEVADA
Las Vegas, Colorado Desert, Needles, San Bernardino, Salton S., Salton Sea, Mexicali, Calexico, Tijuana, Ensenada, B.de Encenada, S. Quintin, Rosario, S.Guadalupe I., B.S. Sebastian Vizcaino, Cedros I., Cerro de la Encantada 10100

Lower Cal.

Sacramento, Berkeley, Stockton, San Francisco, Oakland, San Jose, Santa Cruz, Fresno, Mt.Lyell 13090, Mt.Whitney 14501, Death Valley, Mt.Tyall, Bakersfield, Kern R., Paso Robles, S.Luis Obispo, Santa Barbara Chan., Santa Rosa I., Santa Cruz I., Long Beach, Los Angeles, Santa Catalina I., San Clemente I., San Diego, Channel Islands, Coast Range, Sierra Nevada

PACIFIC OCEAN

Statute Miles
0 50 100 200 300

35, 120, 110, 105, 30

PACIFIC COAST

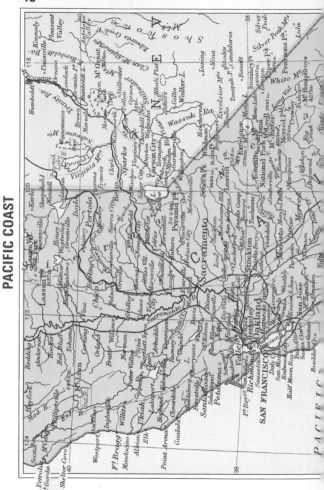

© -John Bartholomew & Son, Ltd. Edinburgh

Death
Lone.pine Valley
Keeler
Owens
Olancha L.

China
L.Maria Thomas

Mt.Whitney
Sumgit Sevt
14418m
Independence
Sierra
Gregy Spring
Johnson
Rankburg
Pinta Pt
Coso
Isabella
Isabella L
Colinte

Mojave Kramer
Maroc Rogers
De
L.
Rosamond
Harold
acton
San Gabriel Ra
Summit
Whiting
Santa Ana

LOS ANGELES
Compton
Redondo B.
San Pedro, Wilmington
San Pedro, Chan.
Long Beach
118

OCEAN

Bay of Monterey
Del.Monte
Pacific Grove
Lake Majella Monterey
Carmel
Jamesburg
Point Sur Sur

Salinas
Castroville

Mendota
Fresno
Clovis
Sanger
Sequoia
National
Park
Visalia
Goshen
Hanford
Lemoore
Porterville

F.
Mt.Whitney

Kernah

Seby

Irvin
Coalinga
Huron
Burris
Lemoore
Tulare R.
Tulare
Corcoran
Delano
Famoso
Elma

McFarland
Ferris Bella
Venturi
Delano

Bakersfield
Tehachapi
Mt.Pinos
2692m

P.Gorda
Bradley
San Ardo
Lucia

King City
San Miguel
Paso Robles
Atascadero
S.Juan
Santa Margarita
S.Luis Obispo
Buena Vista
Fellows
Maricopa

Pt.Piedras Blancos
S.Simeon B.
Cambria
Estero Pt

Morro
San Luis
Port San Luis
Arroyo Grande
Guadalupe
Casmalia
Surf
Rocky Pt
Lompoc
Pt.Concepcion

Los Olivos
Santa Ynez R.
Gaviota
Ellwood
Santa Barbara
Ojai

Ventura
Oxnard
Sta.Monica B.
Santa Monica

Santa Barbara Chan.

San Miguel I.
Sta Cruz I.
Sta.Cruz L.
Sta Barbara L.
SANTA BARBARA
CHANNEL

Sta Rosa I.
Santa Cruz Channel
Begg Rk
Catalina I.
ISLANDS

Statute Miles
0   20   40   60   80   100

36

Statute Miles
50   60   70   80   90   100

124   122   120

WASH.
OREGON

Cumberland
Pt Renfrew
Pt Morris
Victoria
Nanaimo
Juan de Fuca Str.
C.Flattery
Tatoosh
Taholah

Squamish
Howe
Fraser
Vancouver
New Westminster

Hope
Mt Baker
3750m

Sumas
Lynden
Anacortes
Oak Harbor
Everett

Seattle
Olympic
Pen.
Quinault
Hoquiam
Aberdeen
Willapa B.
Oysterville
C.Disappointment
Columbia R.

Mt Olympus
McCleary
Elma
Centralia
Chehalis

Mt Rainier
4277m
Tacoma
Puget Sd.
Olympia

Ellensburg
Yakima
Toppenish
Yakima R.

Goldendale
The Dalles
Arlington
Portland
Mt Hood

Tillamook
Hillsboro

0

34

50   60   70   80   90   100

ALASKA

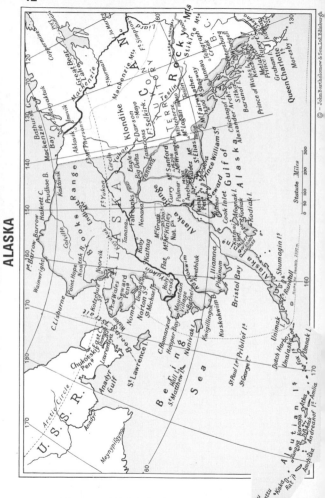

© — John Bartholomew & Son, Ltd. Edinburgh

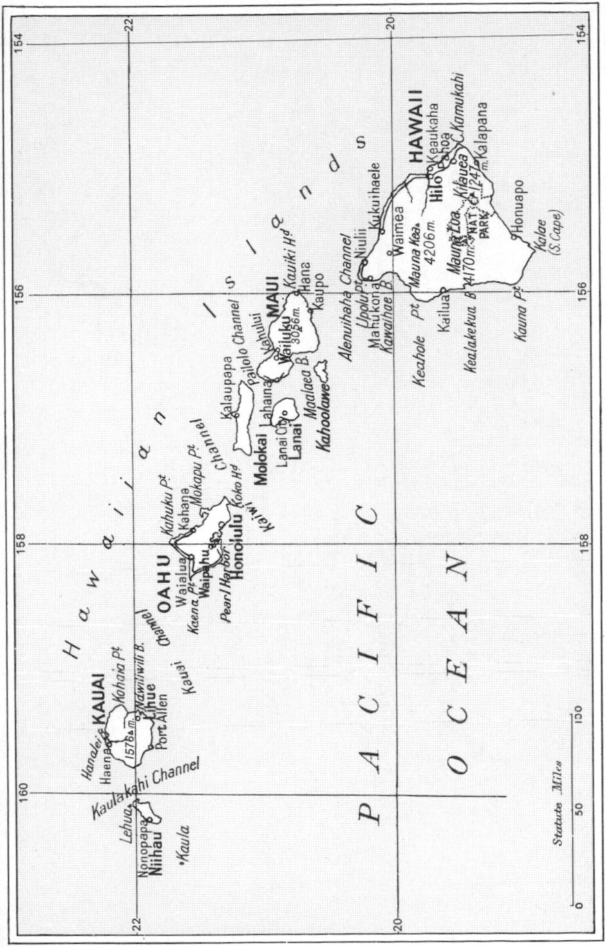
Hawaiian Islands
PACIFIC OCEAN
KAUAI
Hanalei
Haena
Kohala Pt
1576 m.
Nawiliwili B.
Lihue
Port Allen
Kaulakahi Channel
Lehua
Nonopapa
Niihau
Kaula
Kauai Channel
OAHU
Kaena Pt
Waialua
Waipahu
Pearl Harbor
Honolulu
Kahuku Pt
Kahana
Mokapu Pt
Koko Hd
Kaiwi Channel
Molokai
Kalaupapa
Pailolo Channel
Lanai City
Lanai
Lahaina
Maalaea B.
Kahoolawe
Kahului
Wailuku
3056 m.
MAUI
Kauiki Hd
Hana
Kaupo
Alenuihaha Channel
Upolu Pt
Mahukona
Kawaihae B.
Niulii
Kukuihaele
Waimea
Mauna Kea
4206 m.
Mauna Loa
4170 m.
NAT. PARK
Kilauea
1247 m.
HAWAII
Hilo
Keaukaha
Olaa
C. Kamukahi
Kalapana
Honuapo
Kalae (S. Cape)
Keahole Pt
Kailua
Kealakekua B.
Kauna Pt
Statute Miles
0
50
100
154
156
158
160
20
22

MEXICO AND C. AMERICA

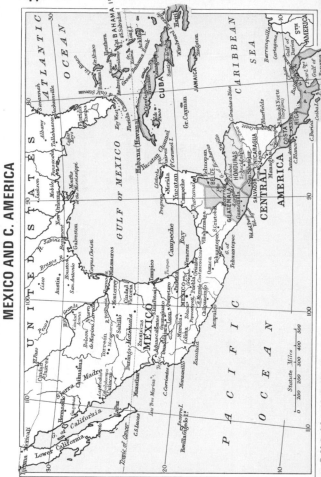

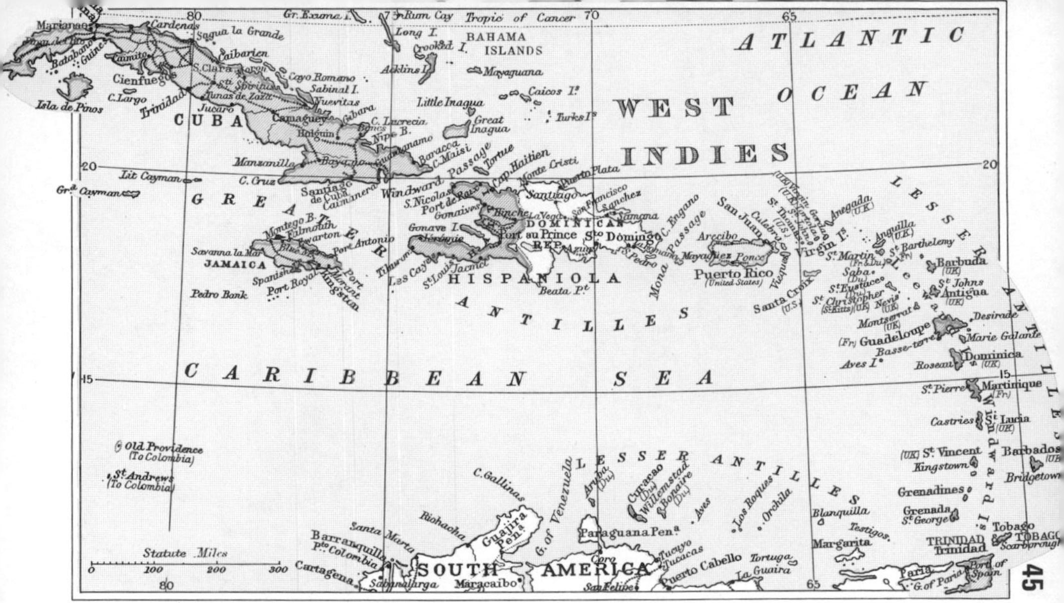

ATLANTIC OCEAN
WEST INDIES
Tropic of Cancer
BAHAMA ISLANDS
Gr. Exuma I.
Rum Cay
Long I.
Crooked I.
Acklins I.
Mayaguana
Caicos Is.
Turks Is.
Little Inagua
Great Inagua
CUBA
Marianao
Cardenas
Sagua la Grande
Caibarien
S. Clara
Cienfuegos
Batabano
C. Largo
Isla de Pinos
Trinidad
Jucaro
Tunas de Zaza
Cayo Romano
Sabinal I.
Nuevitas
Camaguey
Gibara
C. Lucrecia
Nipe B.
Holguin
Manzanillo
Bayamo
Guantanamo
Baracoa
C. Maisi
C. Cruz
Santiago de Cuba
Caimanera
Lit Cayman
Grd. Cayman
GREATER ANTILLES
JAMAICA
Montego B.
Falmouth
Savanna la Mar
Port Antonio
Spanish Town
Port Royal
Kingston
Port Morant
Pedro Bank
Windward Passage
Tortue
Cap Haitien
Monte Cristi
Puerto Plata
S. Nicolas
Port de Paix
Gonaives
Gonave I.
Jérémie
Les Cayes
St. Louis
Jacmel
HISPANIOLA
Hinche
Santiago
La Vega
San Francisco
Sanchez
Samana
DOMINICAN REP.
Port au Prince
Sto. Domingo
Azua
S. Pedro
Beata Pt.
C. Engano
Mona Passage
San Juan
Arecibo
Mayaguez
Ponce
Puerto Rico
(United States)
Culebra
Vieques
Santa Croix (U.S.)
St. Thomas (U.S.)
Virgin Is.
Anegada (U.K.)
LESSER ANTILLES
Anguilla (U.K.)
St. Martin (Fr. & Du.)
St. Bartheleny (Fr.)
Saba (Du.)
St. Eustace (Du.)
St. Christopher (St. Kitts) (UK)
Nevis (UK)
Barbuda (UK)
St. Johns
Antigua (UK)
Montserrat (UK)
(Fr.) Guadeloupe
Basse-terre
Desirade
Marie Galante
Aves I.
Dominica (UK)
Roseau
CARIBBEAN SEA
St. Pierre
Martinique (Fr.)
Castries
St. Lucia (UK)
(UK) St. Vincent
Kingstown
Barbados (UK)
Bridgetown
Windward Is.
Grenadines
Grenada
St. George
Tobago
TRINIDAD & TOBAGO
Trinidad
Scarborough
Port of Spain
Paria
G. of Paria
Old Providence (To Colombia)
St. Andrews (To Colombia)
C. Gallinas
G. of Venezuela
Aruba (Du.)
Curacao (Du.)
Willemstad
Bonaire (Du.)
Aves
Los Roques
Orchila
Blanquilla
Testigos
Margarita
Riohacha
Santa Marta
Barranquilla
Pto. Colombia
Cartagena
Sabanalarga
Guajira Pena.
Maracaibo
Paraguana Pena.
Coro
Tucacas
Tucuyo
Puerto Cabello
Tortuga
La Guaira
San Felipe
SOUTH AMERICA
Statute Miles
0
100
200
300

SOUTH AMERICA

N OCEAN

CENTRAL AMERICA

CARIBBEAN SEA

Gr. Cayman
Jamaica
Hayti Dominica Puerto Rico
C. Gracias a Dios
Guadeloupe
I. W.
Dominica
Martinique
St. Lucia
Barbados
Tobago
TRINIDAD & TOBAGO
Mouths of Orinoco R.
Pt. Gallinas
Cartagena
Barranquilla
S. Marta
Maracaibo
Gulf of Maracaibo
Coro
G. of Darien
G. of Panama
Cocos
Malpelo
Buenaventura
Esmeraldas
Pto. Bolivar
Bahia
C. Blanco
Pta. Aguja
Guayaquil
G. of Guayaquil
Chimborazo
Quito
ECUADOR
Galapagos Is. (Ecu.)

CARACAS
VENEZUELA
Valencia
Trujillo
Bucaramanga
Merida
BOGOTÁ
COLOMBIA
Pasto
Tumaco
Popayan
Cali
Medellin

Cayenne
Paramaribo
Georgetown
C. Orange
New Amsterdam
GUIANA
(DUTCH)
(BRIT.)
(FR.)
Mt. Roraima

Equator
Mouth of Amazon R.
Para
Belem (Para)
Maçapa
R. Araguaia
R. Xingu
R. Tapajos
R. Tocantins
R. Amazon
R. Madeira
R. Purus
R. Roosevelt
R. Branco
Rio Negro
Rio Branco
Manaos
Iquitos

BRAZIL
Campos
Brasilia
Goias
Mato Grosso

Cabo de S. Roque
Natal
Recife
Maceió
Salvador (Bahia)
São Francisco R.
R. São Francisco
Petrolina
Fortaleza
Ceara

PERU
Callao
LIMA
Cuzco
Trujillo
Chiclayo
Arequipa
Andes
El Misti
L. Titicaca
La Paz

OCEAN

VENEZUELA, COLOMBIA, GUIANA

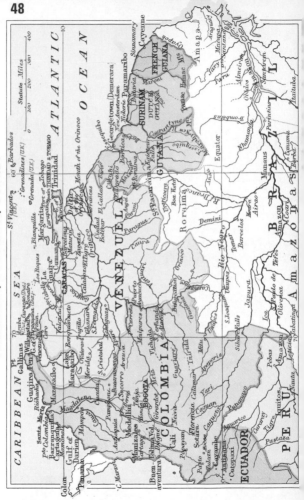

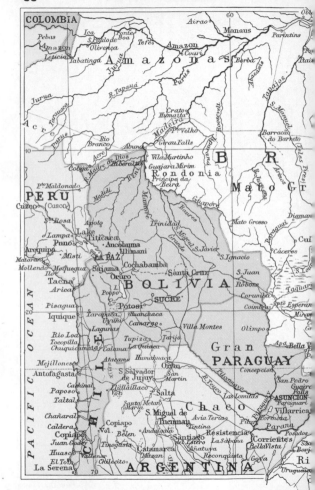

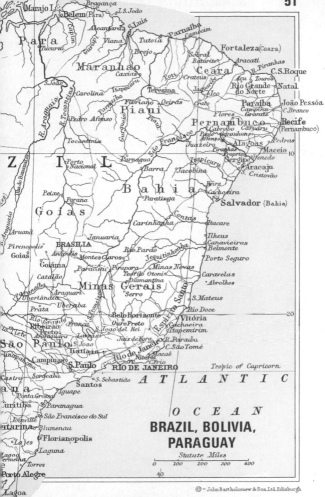

BRAZIL, BOLIVIA,
PARAGUAY

Statute Miles

© – John Bartholomew & Son Ltd. Edinburgh

© · John Bartholomew & Son Ltd. Edinburgh.

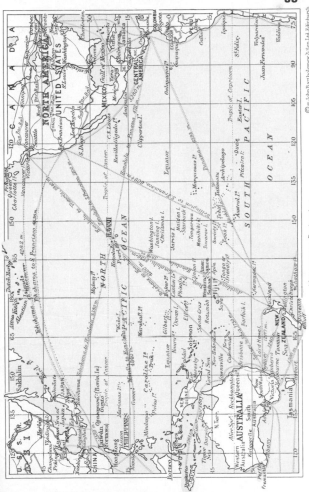

PACIFIC OCEAN

Mercator's Projection

© — John Bartholomew & Son, Ltd, Edinburgh

©John Bartholomew & Son.Ltd.Edinburgh

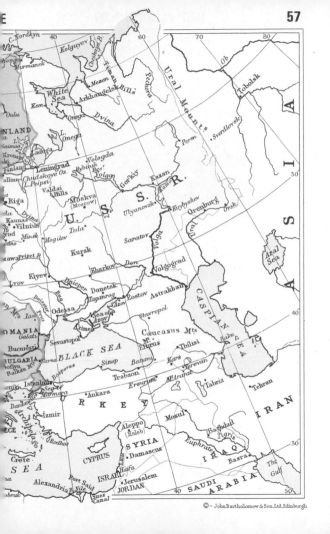

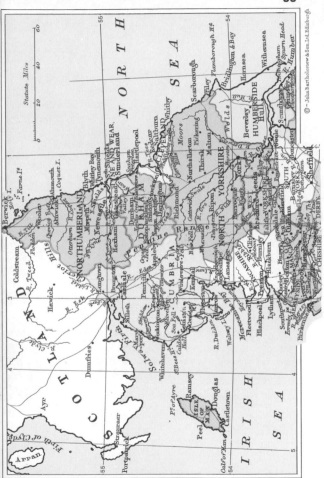

SCOTLAND

Shetland Is.
Yell
Fair I.
Foula
Lerwick
Pomona
Kirkwall
Pentland Firth
Scapa Flow
Statute Miles

Statute Miles
10 20 30 40 50

Buchan Ness
Kinnaird Hd.
Fraserburgh
Peterhead
Aberdeen
Gir-lle-Ness
Stonehaven
Inverbervie
BUCHAN
GRAMPIAN
Cullen
Portsoy
Banff
Turriff
Huntly
Keith
Dufftown-on-Spey
Fochabers
Buckie
Elgin
Forres
Nairn
Ballater
R. Dee
Balmoral
Banchory
R. Don
Strathdon
Ben
Macdui
Braemar
MOUNTAINS
Lossiemouth
Moray Firth
Rothes
Grantown-on-Spey
TAYSIDE

Dunnet Hd.
Duncansby Hd.
Thurso
Wick
Helmsdale
Dornoch Firth
Tain
Cromarty
Dingwall
Beauly
Inverness
Nairn
Kingussie
Aviemore
Loch
Ericht
Loch
Rannoch
Loch
Tummel
Ben
More

Durness
Cape Wrath
Loch Shin
Lairg
SUTHERLAND
Bonar Bridge
HIGHLAND
Loch
Ness
Loch
Lochy
Fort
William
Ben
Nevis
Caledonian Canal

Stromness
Lochinver
Assynt
Ullapool
Loch Broom
Loch Maree
Gairloch
Kinlochewe
Achnasheen
Loch
Carron
Strome Ferry
Kyle of Lochalsh
Mallaig

Pentland Firth
THE MINCH
Little Minch

Butt of Lewis
Stornoway
LEWIS
Harris
OUTER
HEBRIDES
North Uist
Benbecula
South Uist
Barra
Castlebay

Portree
SKYE
Sound of Sleat
Rum
Eigg
Canna
INNER
HEBRIDES

58
57
59
60
58
60
59
2
3
4
5
6
7
8
1

IRELAND

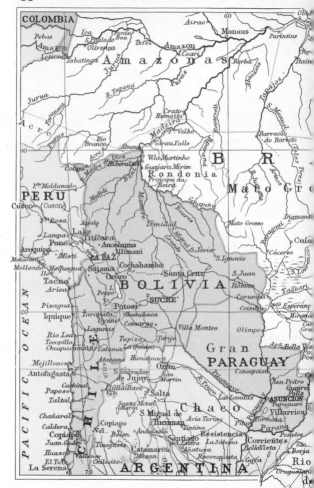

Marajo I.

Bragança ∘I.S.João

Belem (Para)

Para

Capim

Acanjara S.Luis

Viana

Tutoia

Tucurui

Parnahiba Camocim

Pará

Maranhao

Caxias

Fortaleza (Ceara)

Baturite

Aracati

R.Piranhas

C.S.Roque

Sobral

Ceara

Açu Touros

Natal

Rio Grande

do Norte

Crateus

S.João

Carolina

Itapecuru

Teresina

Jaguaribe

Elco

Floriano Oeiras

Piaui

Crato

Flores

Paraiba João Pessõa

Campina C.Branco

Granate

Pedro Afonso

Tocantins

Piaui

Pernambuco

Recife

(Pernambuco)

Cabrobo Caruaru

Paulo Garanhuns

Afonso

Juazeiro

Piranhas

Alagoas

Maceio

Penedo

Proprio

Sergipe

Picuru

Aracaju

S. Cristovão

Porto

Nacional

Parnagua

Barra

Jacobina

Feira

Cachoeira

Salvador (Bahia)

Peixe

Parana

Paratinga

Bahia

Carinhanha

Contas

Itacare

Goias

Januaria

Ilheus

Canavieiras

BRASILIA

Rio Pardo

Jequitinhonha

Belmonte

Aruanã

Andpolis

Montes Claros

Minas Novas

Porto Seguro

Pirenopolis

Goiania

Paracatu

Pirapora

Teofilo Otoni

Caravelas

Goias

Catalão

Diamantina

Abrolhos

Uberlândia

Araguari

Minas Gerais

Serro

S.Mateus

Uberaba

Prata

Belo Horizonte

Vitoria

Rio Doce

Ribeirao

Preto

Ouro Preto

Cachoeira

São Paulos

João del Rei

Itapemirim

R.Paraiba

Campinas

S.João

Juiz de fora

Rio de Janeiro

Incaé

Sorocaba

S.Paulo

Niteroi

C.São Tomé

Santos

RIO DE JANEIRO

C.Frio

Tropic of Capricorn

Castro

PontaGrossa

Iguape

S.Sebastião

ATLANTIC

Curitiba

Paranagua

São Francisco do Sul

OCEAN

Joinville

Blumenau

BRAZIL, BOLIVIA,

Lajes

Florianopolis

PARAGUAY

Lagoa

Vermelha

Torres

Laguna

Statute Miles

Porto Alegre

0   100   200   300   400

40

Lagoa

dos Patos

© ~ John Bartholomew & Son.Ltd.Edinburgh

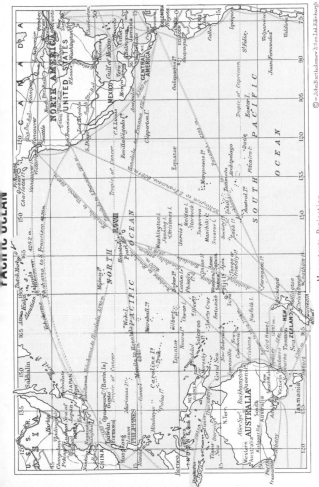

PACIFIC OCEAN

Mercator's Projection

projection

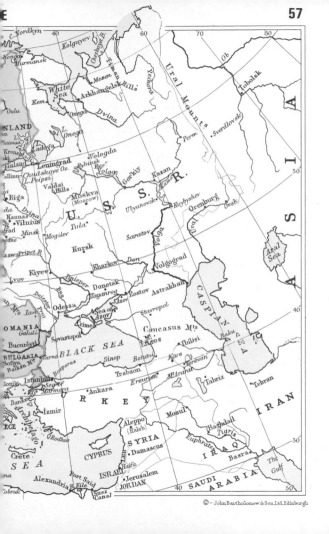

C.Nordkyn
Kolguyev B.
Ob
Tobolsk
Ural Mounts.
Chëshskaya B.
Pechora
Timan Hills
Marmansk
Kenga
Mezen
Archangelsk
White Sea
Dvina
Kem
Omega
Oulu
L.Onega
Perm
Sverdlovsk
U. S. S. R.
L.Saimaa
Vologda
Kama
FINLAND
Kronstadt
Leningrad
Rybinsk
Volga
Kazan
Orenburg
Orsk
Helsinki
L.Ladoga
Yaroslavl
Gorky
Kuybyshev
Tallinn
L.Peipsi
Valdai Hills
Moskva (Moscow)
Ulyanovsk
Ural R.
Aral Sea
Riga
Drina
Kaunas
Vilnius
Minsk
Mogilev
Tula
Saratov
Volga
grad
Pripet R.
Kursk
Warsaw
Lvov
Kiyev
Dnieper
Kharkov
Don
Volgograd
Dniester
Bug
Donetsk
Astrakhan
CASPIAN
Taganrog
Rostov
Ias
Prut
Odessa
Sea of Azov
Stavropol
ROMANIA
Galati
Crimea
Bucuresti
Sevastopol
Caucasus Mts.
Baku
BULGARIA
Varna
Elbrus
Tbilisi
Sofiya
Balkan Mts.
BLACK SEA
Sinop
Batumi
Kars
SEA
loniki
Bosporus
Trabzon
Yerevan
Istanbul
Marmara
Erzurum
Mt.Ararat
Tabriz
Dardanelles
Ankara
T U R K E Y
Tehran
İzmir
GREECE
Archipelago
Rodhos
Aleppo (Haleb)
Mosul
IRAN
Crete
CYPRUS
SYRIA
Baghdad
Tigris
Euphrates
SEA
Damascus
Haifa
ISRAEL
Jerusalem
JORDAN
I R A Q
Basra
The Gulf
Tobruk
Alexandria
Port Said
R.Nile
Suez Canal
SAUDI ARABIA

© - John Bartholomew & Son, Ltd. Edinburgh

© – John Bartholomew & Son. Ltd. Edinburgh

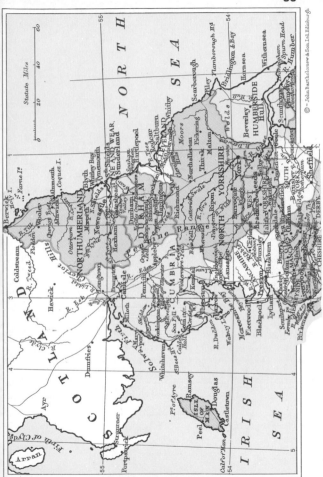

© – John Bartholomew & Son.Ltd.Edinburgh

Statute Miles

NORTH SEA

IRISH SEA

SCOTLAND

NORTHUMBERLAND

DURHAM

TYNE AND WEAR

CLEVELAND

CUMBRIA

NORTH YORKSHIRE

LANCASHIRE

WEST YORKSHIRE

HUMBERSIDE

SOUTH YORKSHIRE

MERSEYSIDE

CHESHIRE

GREATER MANCHESTER

DERBY.

ISLE OF MAN

Firth of Clyde

Arran

Berwick

Coldstream

Hawick

Dumfries

Ayr

Stranraer

Portpatrick

Pt.of Ayre

Ramsey

Peel

Douglas

Castletown

Cal.of Man

Carlisle

Penrith

Appleby

Kendal

Whitehaven

Workington

Maryport

Keswick

Barrow

Morecambe

Fleetwood

Blackpool

Lytham

Southport

Formby Pt.

Liverpool

Birkenhead

Preston

Blackburn

Burnley

Bolton

Bury

Wigan

Warrington

Manchester

Stockport

Macclesfield

Crewe

Chester

Northwich

Sheffield

Rotherham

Barnsley

Doncaster

Leeds

Bradford

Halifax

Huddersfield

Wakefield

Dewsbury

Harrogate

York

Selby

Ripon

Northallerton

Thirsk

Malton

Pickering

Scarborough

Filey

Bridlington & Bay

Flamborough Hd.

Hornsea

Withernsea

Beverley

Hull

Grimsby

Cleethorpes

Spurn Head

R. Humber

Whitby

Saltburn

Redcar

Hartlepool

Middlesbrough

Stockton

Darlington

Durham

Sunderland

S. Shields

N. Shields

Tynemouth

Newcastle

Gateshead

Whitley Bay

Blyth

Morpeth

Ashington

Alnwick

Rothbury

Wooler

Bamborough

Holy I.

Farne Is.

Coquet I.

Berwick

R. Tweed

Flodden

Cheviot Hills

R. Till

The Cheviot

R. Coquet

R. Wansbeck

R. Tyne

Hexham

Bellingham

R. N. Tyne

Pennine Range

Cross Fell

R. Eden

R. Lune

R. Ribble

Skiddaw

Sca Fell

Windermere

Ullswater

R. Derwent

St. Bees Hd.

Walney I.

Morecambe Bay

Cleveland Hills

Cleveland

Cleveland Moors

York Moors

Wolds

Vale of York

R. Ure

R. Swale

Richmond

Catterick

Wensleydale

Swaledale

Wharfedale

Airedale

R. Aire

R. Wharfe

R. Calder

R. Don

R. Trent

R. Ouse

R. Derwent

R. Dee

R. Mersey

R. Weaver

R. Tees

R. Wear

NORTH

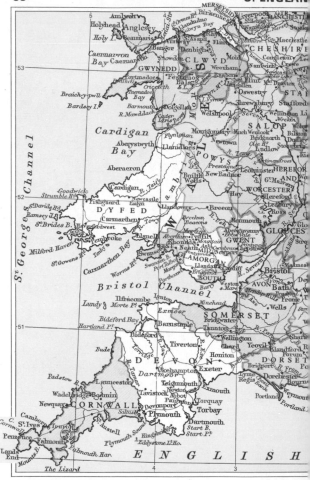

SCOTLAND

NORTH

N

Arbroath
Forfar
Dundee
St Andrews
Fife Ness
FIFE
Firth of Tay
Dunkeld Blairgowrie
R. Tay
Cupar
Perth
TAYSIDE
Crieff
Comrie
Dunblane
Ochil Hills
Kinross L. Leven
Dunfermline
North Berwick
Dunbar
Firth of Forth
LOTHIAN
Dalkeith
Lammermuir Hills
Abbs Hd
Berwick upon Tweed
Duns
Coldstream
Greenlaw
Kelso
R. Tweed
BORDERS
Jedburgh
Hawick
Cheviot Hills
ENGLAND

L. Rannoch
Loch Tay
L. Earn
Callander
L. Katrine
L. Lomond
CENTRAL
Stirling
Falkirk
Bo'ness
Linlithgow
Bathgate
R. Forth
Kincardine
Alloa

GRAMPIAN

Glasgow
Paisley
Hamilton
Motherwell
Cumbernauld
Kilsyth
Lanark
Peebles
Galashiels
Selkirk
Melrose
St Boswells
Newtown St Boswells
Moffat
R. Tweed
Innerleithen

DUMFRIES AND GALLOWAY
Dumfries
Langholm
R. Nith
Lockerbie
R. Esk
Annan
Carlisle
R. Eden
Solway Firth
Sanquhar
R. Dee
New Galloway
Kirkcudbright
Castle Douglas
R. Nith

Tobermory
Staffa
Iona
Tiree
Mull
Oban
L. Awe
L. Etive
L. Linnhe
L. Fyne
STRATHCLYDE
Inveraray
Dunoon
Gourock
Greenock
Largs
Ardrossan
Irvine
Kilmarnock
Ayr
Prestwick
Troon
Firth of Clyde
Rothesay
Bute
Arran
Brodick
Lamlash
Ailsa Craig
Girvan
Dalbeattie
Stranraer
Portpatrick
Luce Bay
Wigtown B.
Wigtown
Mull of Galloway
New Galloway

INNER
Colonsay
Jura
Islay
Port Ellen
Sound of Jura
Kintyre
Campbeltown
Mull of Kintyre

North Channel

IRISH SEA

IRELAND
Belfast
Londonderry

ATLANTIC OCEAN

© John Bartholomew & Son. Ltd. Edinburgh.

IRELAND

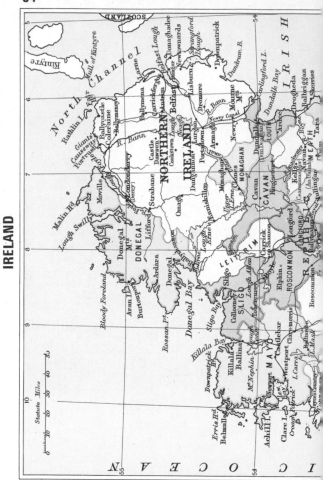

SCANDINAVIA

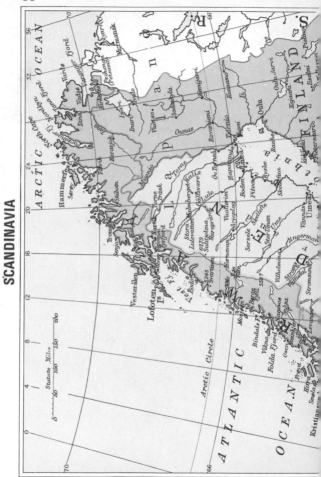

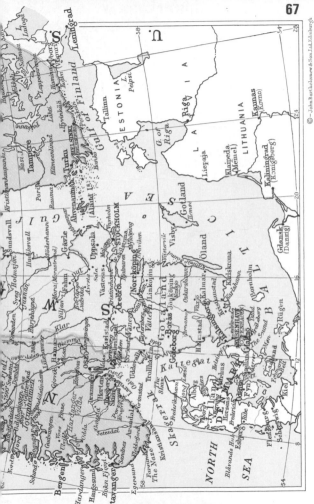

Statute Miles

ATLANTIC

OCEAN

Namsos

N.Trøndelag

Oksbås

Froan

Frøya
Hitra
Smøla

Kristiansund
Averøy
Bud
Gossen
Molde

Romsdal
Ålesund
Hareidland
Stadland
Peninsula
Nordf.
Bremanger
Frøysjöen
Florø
Stav Fj.
Dalsf.
Solund
Husöy
Sogne Fjord
Fens Fj.
Radö
Holsen
Sotra
Bjørne
Bergen
Storö
Bomlo
Bömlö Fj.
Haugesund
Karmøy
Røkn Fj.
Stavanger

Møre og Romsdal

Dovre
Fjell
Snøhetta
7500

Trondheim
S.Trøndelag
Sylene
5780
Røros

Hedmark
Sånfjället
4189

Opland
Lillehammer

Hamar
Mjøsa

S
W
E
D
E
N

Sogn og Fjordane

Galdhøpig
8100
Jotun
Glittertind
8104
heimen

Buskerud

Akershus

OSLO

Oslo

Telemark

Vest-
Agder

Aust-
Agder

Rogaland

Østfold
Fredrikstad

Kristiansand

Lindesnes
(The Naze)

SKAGERRAK

Göteborg
(Gothenburg)

DENMARK

© — John Bartholomew & Son, Ltd. Edinburgh

© - John Bartholomew & Son, Ltd. Edinburgh.

NETHERLANDS. BELGIUM, LUXEMBOURG

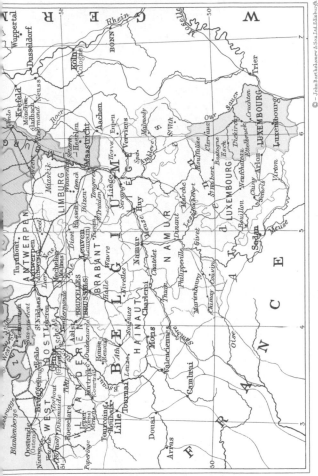

ENGLAND

ENGLISH CHANNEL

Dover

Calai

Boulogne

Montreuil

St Valery

Dieppe

Fécamp

Rouen

Elbeuf

Evreux

Le Havre

Caen

St Lo

Argentan

Alençon

Le Mans

Mayenne

Laval

Rennes

Fougeres

Avranches

Granville

St Malo

Dinan

Servan

St Brieuc

Pontivy

Brittany

Quimper

Lorient

Vannes

Belle Ile

St Nazaire

R. Loire

I. Noirmoutier

I. d'Yeu

Les Sables d'Olonne

I. de Ré

La Rochelle

L. d'Oléron

Rochefort

Royan

Pauillac

Blaye

Arcachon

Bordeaux

Bazas

Landes

Bayonne

Biarritz

Dax

Santander

San Sebastian

Bilbao

Ebro

Pamplona

SPAIN

Perdido

Maladeta

Andorra

Plymouth

Falmouth

Lands End

Isles of Scilly

Portsmouth

C. de la Hague

Alderney

Guernsey

Sark

Jersey

Channel Islands

Pt de Talbert

Morlaix

I. de Ouessant (Ushant I.)

Brest

Pt St Mathieu

I. de Sein

Versai

Chartres

Maine

Orle

Loir

Loire

Tours

Blois

Angers

Anjou

Nantes

Saumur

Chinon

Châteaubriant

Vilaine

Poitou

Châtellerault

Poitiers

Vienne

Niort

Civray

Argenton

St Julien

Saintes

Cognac

Angoulême

Périgueux

Brive

Tulle

Limog

Libourne

Bergerac

Dordogne

Villeneuve s. Lot

Cahors

Agen

Mont de Marsan

Auch

Muret

Toul

Orthez

Pau

Tarbes

Carcas

Oloron

Foix

Lus

Andorra

BAY OF BISCAY

Statute Miles
0   50   100

50

48

46

44

Gironde

Garonne

Gascony

Pyrenees

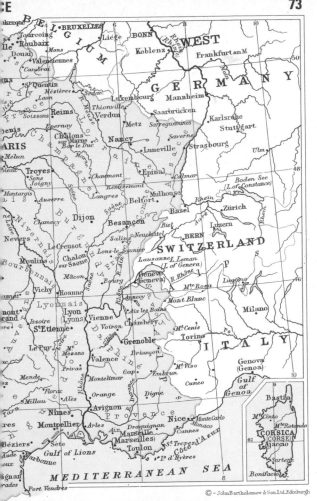

© – John Bartholomew & Son Ltd. Edinburgh.

SWITZERLAND

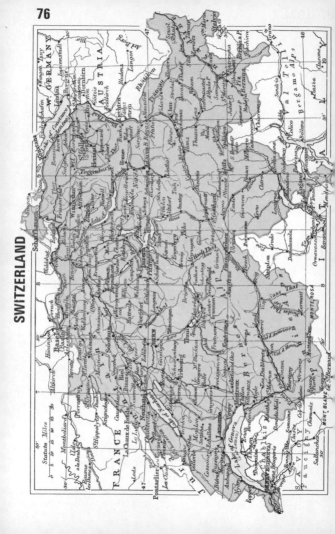

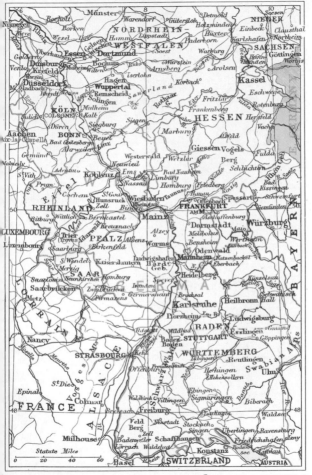

Statute Miles
0   20   40   60

© – John Bartholomew & Son. Ltd. Edinburgh.

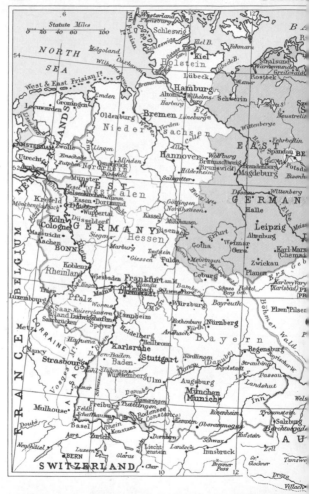

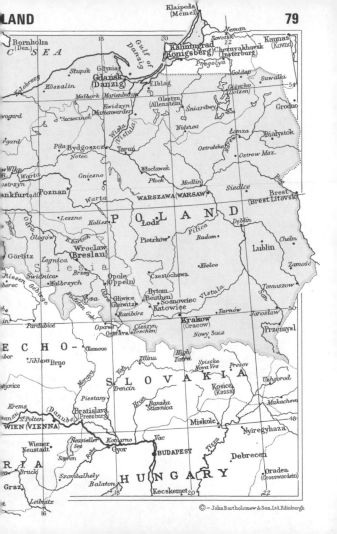

Klaipeda (Memel)

Bornholm (Den.)

C SEA

Neman

Soretsk

Kaunas (Kovno)

Stupsk Gdynia

Gulf of Danzig

Kaliningrad Königsberg

Chernyakhovsk (Insterburg)

Pregolya

Goldap

Suwalki

Gdansk (Danzig)

Elbląg

Koszalin

Malbork Marienburg

Olsztyn (Allenstein)

Gizycko (Lötzen)

vogard

Suczecinek

Kwidzyn Marienwerder

Śniardwy

Grodno

gard

Wlkp

Pila Bydgoszcz

Notec

Toruń

Nidzica

Łomża

Białystok

Ostroleka

Ostrow Maz.

*frankfurt*a

Poznan

Gniezno

Warta

Włocławek

Płock

Modlin

Narew

Siedlce

Brest (Brest Litovsk)

Leszno

Kalisz

P O L A N D

Łódź

Warta

Glogow

R.Barycz

Wrocław (Breslau)

Piotrków

Pilica

Radom

Dęblin

Chełm

Görlitz

Legnica

Silesia

Świdnica

Brzeg

Opole (Oppeln)

Kielce

Lublin

Zamość

Riesen Gebirge

Wałbrzych

Nysa

Częstochowa

berec

Glatzer Geb.

Gliwice Gleiwitz

Bytom Beuthen

Sosnowice

Katowice

Vistula

Tomaszow

San

in

Pardubice

Opava

Raciborz

Cieszyn Teschen

Kraków (Cracow)

Tarnów

Jarosław

Przemysl

E C H O −

Olomouc

Ostrava

Nowy Sacz

bor

Jihlava

Brno

Morava

Žilina

High Tatra

Spisska Nova Ves

Presov

Uzhgorod

S L O V A K I A

jovice

Vah

Trencin

Hron

Kosice (Kassa)

Mukachevo

Krems

St Polten

Danube

Piestany

Banska Stiavnica

WIEN (VIENNA)

Bratislava (Pressburg)

Miskolc

Nyiregyhaza

Wiener Neustadt

Neusiedler See

Komarno

Vac

BUDAPEST

Debrecen

Sopron

Gyor

Raab

RIA

Bruck

Szombathely

Balaton

H U N G A R Y

Oradea (Grosswardein)

Graz

Leibnitz

Kecskemet

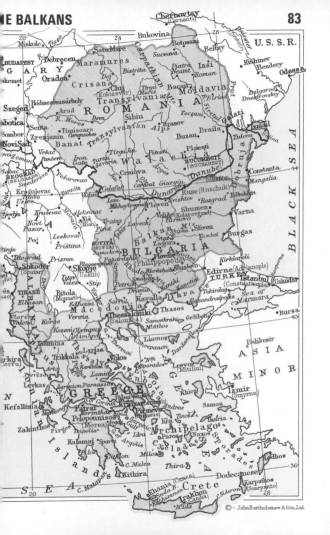

NORTH ITALY

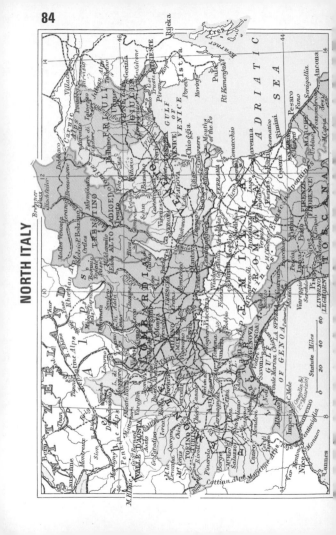

WESTERN U.S.S.R.

U. S. S. R.

Ural Mountains

Timan Range

BARENTS SEA

WHITE SEA

Kola Peninsula

Murman Coast

LAPLAND

NORWAY

SWEDEN

FINLAND

Gulf of Bothnia

Gulf of Finland

BALTIC SEA

ESTONIA

LATVIA

LITHUANIA

Leningrad

HELSINKI

STOCKHOLM

Tallinn

Riga

Arctic Circle

Kara Sea

Kara Str.

Vaygach I.

Yugor Str.

Kolguev I.

Pechora

Pechora R.

N. Dvina

Lake Onega

Lake Ladoga

North Cape

Kanin Pen.

Arkhangelsk

Mezen

Onega

Narva

Pskov

Moscow

Yaroslavl

Vologda

Kostroma

Ivanovo

Kalinin

Novgorod

Pinega

Izhma

Sukhona

Vaga

Pskov

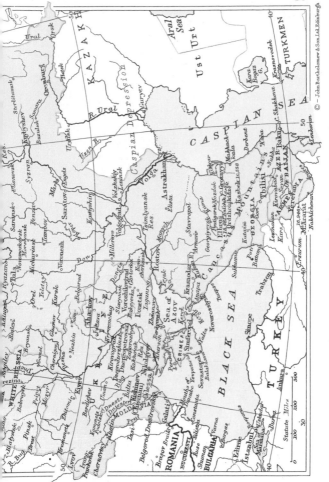

© – John Bartholomew & Son Ltd.Edinburgh

UKRAINE

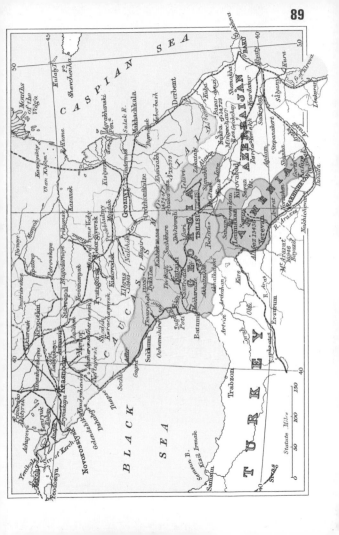

SOVIET CENTRAL ASIA

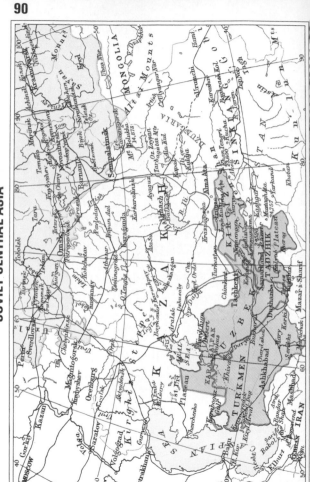

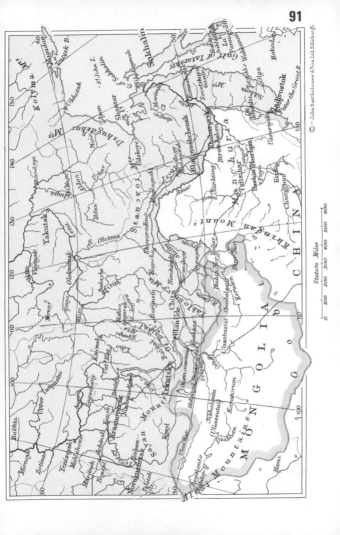

© – John Bartholomew & Son, Ltd, Edinburgh.

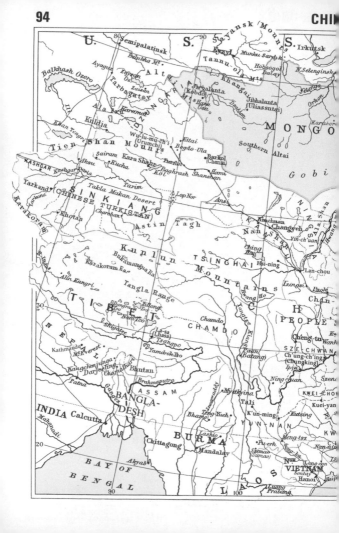

U. <u>80</u> S. Semipalatinsk <u>90</u> Sayansk Mounts. Irkutsk

Belukha Mt. Kyzyl Munku Sardyk N.Selenginsk

Balkhash Ozero Ayaguz Zaysan Tannu-ola Hobsogol Dalay Yeleroy

Tarbagatay Uzbek Zaisan Khangai Mts Jibhalanta (Iliassutu) Orkon Karukhon

Ala-Shan Karaman Urgalanta Kobdo Ms Hangi Uot Dzerban MONGO

Khan Tengri Kuldja Wu-lu-mu-ch'i (Urumchi) Kitai Begdo-Ula Southern Altai Gobi

Tien Shan Mounts Sairam Kara Shahr Barkol (Chensi)

KASHGAR Iksu Kucha Baghrash Kol Hami Shanshan

Yarkand Kashgar Yarim Lop Nor Ansi

Karakoram SINKIANG (CHINESE TURKISTAN) Takla Makan Desert Ansi

Khotan Cherchen Astin Tagh Kan-chau Changyeh Yin-ch'uan

K u n l u n TSINGHAI Ching Hai Hsi-ning Lan-chou

Karakoram Ra. Mountains Liangsi Paoki

Alin Kangri Tangla Range Hwang Ho Cha

T I B E T Zilong Chamdo Yangtze Kiang CHEng-tu

NEPAL Lhasa Tsangpo CHAMDO SZECHWAN Ch'ung-ch'ing (Chungking)

Kathmandu Mt.Everest Yamdrok Tso Ning-yuan KWEI-CHO

Kangchenjunga Shigatse Batang KWEI-CHOW Kuei-yang

Darjeeling Chumbi Bhutan Ipin

INDIA Patna Brahmaputra ASSAM Myitkyina Tali Kiating

BANGLA-DESH Ganges Bhamo Ting-Yüeh YUNNAN K'un-ming Meng-tsz

Calcutta Mahanadi Lashio Pu-erh Ssemao (Sumao)

Chittagong Akyab BURMA Mandalay VIETNAM

BAY OF BENGAL <u>90</u> LAOS Luang Prabang <u>100</u> Hanoi

JAPAN

SEA OF JAPAN

HONSHU

SOUTH KOREA

PACIFIC OCEAN

SHIKOKU

KYŪSHŪ

KOREA STR.

Tsushima Str.

Bungo Str.

Suō Nada

Iyo Nada

Tosa Bay

Osaka Bay

Wakasa Bay

Toyama Bay

Ise Bay

Sado I.

Oki gunto

Nishi-sh.

Nakano-sh.

Takeshima

Noto Penin.

Nanao

Kanazawa

Komatsu

Fukui

Tsuruga

Gifu

Nagoya

Kyōto

Ōsaka

Kōbe

Nara

Yokohama

Tōkyō

Chiba

Nikkō

Shizuoka

Hamamatsu

Hiroshima

Okayama

Matsue

Hamada

Hagi

Shimonoseki

Fukuoka

Nagasaki

Kumamoto

Kagoshima

Miyazaki

Ōita

Takamatsu

Tokushima

Kōchi

Matsuyama

Goto Retto

Amakusa-sh.

Tsushima

Iki

Pusan

Masan

Taegu

Ullŭng Do (Dagelet)

Statute Miles

0   50   100   150

Bonin Is. (Ogasawara)

Izu Shichi to

Ō-shima

Miyake-jima

Mikura-jima

Hachijo-jima

Koshima-

Aoga-sh.

130   135   140

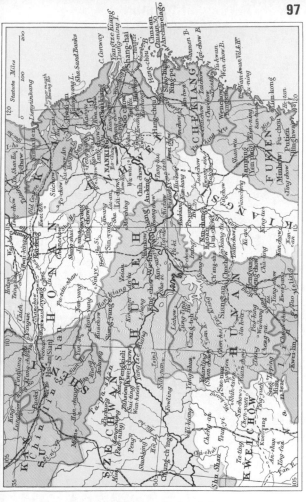

© —John Bartholomew & Son.Ltd.Edinburgh

MARIANAS

Pagan
Guguan
Anatahan I.
Saipan
Tinian
Rota (U.S.)
Guam (U.S.)

CAROLINE ISLANDS
U.S. Trust Terr.
Kusaie
Ngulu
Fais
Truk
Ponapé
Faraulep
Woleai
Lamotrek
Eauripik
U.S. Trust Terr.

Yap
Palau
Babelthuap

Challenger
Deep 35,187ft.

P A C I F I C   O C E A N

Equator

Sonsorol I.
Helen Reef

Morotai
Waigeo
Mapia Is.

Ninigo Is.
Admiralty Is.
Mussau
Bismarck Archipelago
New Ireland
New Britain

Pt. d'Urville
Humboldt B.
Sarmi
Biak
Nabire
Japen
Waropen
Wewak

NEW GUINEA
PAPUA
Madang
Lae
Gulf
Port Moresby

Markham
Bulolo
Kikori
Kerema

New Georgia I.
Santa Isabel I.
Malaita
Solomon
Islands
Bougainville
Buka
Guadalcanal
San Cristobal
Rennell I.

CORAL SEA

Thursday I.
Torres Strait
Cape York

Samarai
Mt. Albert Edward
Milne B.

IRIAN JAYA
P. Jaja
Kaimana
Fak Fak
Etna B.
Merauke
Kolepom

ARAFURA SEA

Aru Is.
Kai Is.
Tanimbar Is.
Timorlaut I.

MOLUCCAS
Halmahera
Ternate
Sula Is.
Buru
Ceram
Ambon
Banda Is.
BANDA SEA

Manado
CELEBES SEA
SULAWESI
Kendari

Makassar
(Ujung Pandang)

TIMOR SEA

Melville I.
Darwin

AUSTRALIA

PHILIPPINES
B. Buyan Is.
C. Engaño
Luzon
Palanan Pt.
Polillo
Manila
Mindoro
Samar
Panay
Negros
Leyte
Cebu
Bohol
Mindanao
Zamboanga
Davao
Surigao
Basilan
SULU SEA
Jolo
Sandakan

Hainan I.
S O U T H E R N
C H I N A   S E A

T H A I L A N D
Rangoon
Moulmein
Krung Thep
(Bangkok)
Gulf of
Thailand
KHMER
REP.
VIET NAM
LAOS
INDO-CHINA
Cochin-China
Saigon

Malay Peninsula
MALAYSIA
BRUNEI
SABAH
SARAWAK
Kuala Lumpur
Singapore
Kuching
Banjarmasin
KALIMANTAN
B O R N E O

I N D O N E S I A
Sumatera
Padang
Palembang
Jakarta
J A V A
Bandung
Surabaya
Semarang

Sunda Str.
Bali
Lombok
Sumbawa
Flores
Flores Sea
Sumba
Sawu
Roti
Timor

I N D I A N   O C E A N

Statute Miles

© – John Bartholomew & Son Ltd. Edinburgh

5571

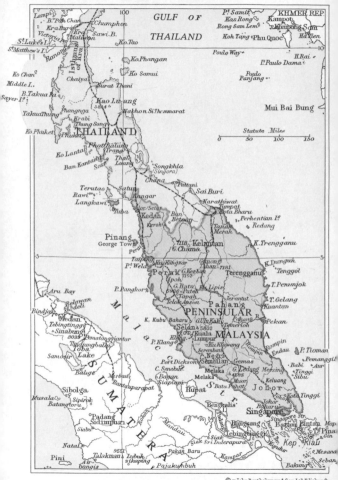

GULF OF
THAILAND

KHMER REP

THAILAND

PENINSULAR

MALAYSIA

SUMATERA

Singapore

Statute Miles

0   50   100   150

©—John Bartholomew & Son Ltd. Edinburgh

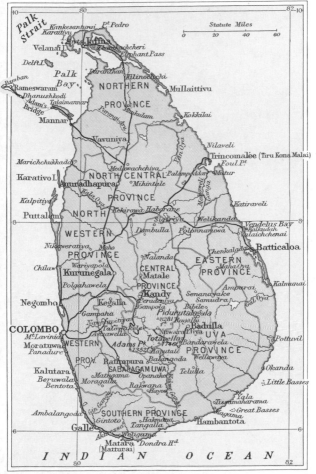

Palk Strait
Kankesanturai
Karaitivu
Pt Pedro
Velanai I.
Fort Jaffna
Chankachcheri
Delft I.
Elephant Pass
Pamban
Rameswaram
Dhanushkodi
Adam's
Bridge
Talaimanar
Mannar
Palk Bay
Paranthan
Kilinochchi
Mullaittivu
NORTHERN
PROVINCE
Pukulam
Kokkilai
Vavuniya
Nilaveli
Marichchukkadd.
Medawachchiya
Palampiddam
Trincomalee (Tiru Kona Malai)
Foul Pt
Mutur
Karativo I.
NORTH CENTRAL
Mihintale
Anuradhapura
Yan Oya
Kalpitiya
Kala Oya
PROVINCE
Katiraveli
Puttalam
NORTH
Kekirawa
Habarane
Sigiriya
Welikanda
Vendelus Bay
WESTERN
Dambulla
Polonnaruwa
Kalkudah
Valaichchenai
Nikaweratiya
Maho
Chenkalady
Batticaloa
PROVINCE
Wariyapola
Nalanda
EASTERN
Chilaw
Kurunegala
CENTRAL
Matale
PROVINCE
Maha Oya
Kalmunai
Polgahawela
PROVINCE
Amparai
Gal Oya
Negombo
Kegalla
Kandy
Senanayake
Gampaha
Peradeniya
Samudra
Bibile
COLOMBO
Ruanwella
Gampola
Pidurutalagala
Badulla
Mt Lavinia
Avissawella
Nuwara Eliya
Pottuvil
Moratuwa
WESTERN
Adams Pk
Totapella
UVA
Panadure
PROV.
Ratnapura
Bandarawela
PROVINCE
Kalutara
SABARAGAMUWA
Balangoda
Wellawaya
Beruwala
Matugama
Opanake
Telulla
Okanda
Bentota
Moragalla
Rakwana
Little Basses
Hayes
Ambalangoda
SOUTHERN PROVINCE
Yala
Tissamaharama
Great Basses
Galle
Gintoto
Hakmana
Magama
Hambantota
Weligama
Tangalla
Matara (Matturai)
Dondra Hd

Statute Miles
0   20   40   60

I N D I A N   O C E A N

© – John Bartholomew & Son Ltd. Edinburgh

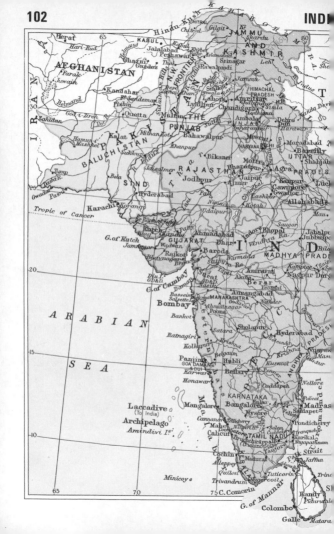

UTTAR PRADESH

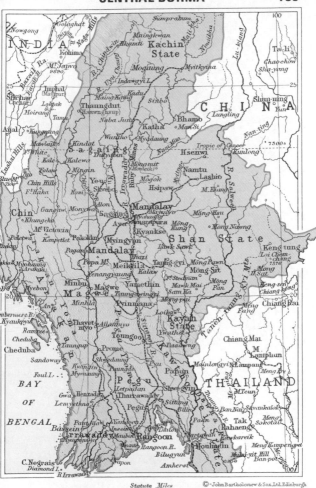

Statute Miles
0   50   100   150

©-John Bartholomew & Son, Ltd. Edinburgh

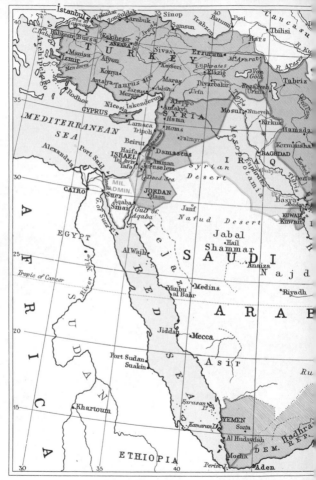

TURKEY

AFRICA

ATLANTIC OCEAN

EUROPE

ASIA

Lisbon
Paris

Black Sea

Istanbul
Ankara

Caspian Sea

MEDITERRANEAN SEA

Cyprus
Jerusalem

SAUDI ARABIA

Mecca
Medina

RED SEA

Port Said
Suez
Cairo
Alexandria Damietta
Asyût
Aswân

ARAB REP. OF EGYPT

Libyan Desert

Nile

Tripoli
Tunis
TUNISIA
Annaba
Algiers
Oran

MOROCCO
Rabat
Casablanca
Fès
Marrakech
Essaouira

Strait of Gibraltar
Ceuta

Madeira (P.)
Canary Is.
Tenerife (Sp.)

ALGERIA
Ouargla
Béchar
Adrar

LIBYA
Fezzan
Murzuq
Ghat

Tibesti
Zouar
CHAD
L. Chad

NIGER
Agadès
Zinder

SAHARA
Tropic of Cancer
Ahaggar
Tamanrasset
In Salah

MAURITANIA
Atar
Nouâdhibou
Villa Cisneros
C. Bojador

SPANISH SAHARA

MALI
SEGOU
Timbouctou
Gao

SENEGAL
St-Louis
R. Senegal
Dakar

Bissau
PORTUGUESE GUINEA
Banjul
THE GAMBIA

SIERRA LEONE

UPPER VOLTA

NIGERIA
Sokoto
Kano
Kaduna
Kumo

DAHOMEY
TOGO

IVORY COAST

SUDAN
Khartoum
El Obeid
El Fasher
Nyala
Dongola
Port Sudan
Kassala

ERITREA
Asmara
Massawa

Addis Ababa
Harar
Djibouti

Socotra I.
Aden
Gouralahti

Darnah
Benghazi

80 70 60 50 40 30 20 10

OCEAN

INDIAN OCEAN

ATLANTIC OCEAN

Gulf of Guinea

Equator

Tropic of Capricorn

ZAIRE

ANGOLA

ZAMBIA

RHODESIA

BOTSWANA

South West AFRICA (NAMIBIA)

SOUTH AFRICA

TANZANIA

KENYA

MALAWI

MOZAMBIQUE

MALAGASY REP. (MADAGASCAR)

Mozambique Channel

SWAZILAND

NATAL

TRANSVAAL

ORANGE FREE STATE

CAPE of GOOD HOPE

GABON

CONGO

Kinshasa

Brazzaville

Libreville

Francoville

São Tomé

Annobon

Ascension I. (U.K.)

St. Helena I. (U.K.)

Tristan da Cunha (U.K.)

England to The Cape 5950 Miles

Cape Town

Cape of Good Hope

C. Agulhas

Port Elizabeth

East London

Durban

Pietermaritzburg

Bloemfontein

Johannesburg

Pretoria

Lourenço Marques

Lüderitz

Walvis Bay

Swakopmund

Windhoek

Kalahari Desert

Bulawayo

Salisbury

Lusaka

Livingstone

Nova Lisboa

Benguela

Lobito

Loanda

Moçamedes

C. Frio

Luanda

Elisabethville (Lubumbashi)

Kananga

Lake Tanganyika

L. Nyasa

L. Mweru

Dar es Salaam

Zanzibar

Mombasa

Malindi

Nairobi

Dodoma

Tabora

Tanga

Nampula

Beira

Inhambane

Nyala

Nampula

Antananarivo

Tamatave

C. St. Marie

Mogadiscio

Statute Miles
0 100 200 300 400 500

© - John Bartholomew & Son, Ltd., Edinburgh

EGYPT, LIBYA

ARAB REP. OF EGYPT

MEDITERRANEAN SEA

RED SEA

SYRIA
JORDAN
SAUDI ARABIA
ISRAEL
Cyprus
TUNISIA
ALGERIA
NIGER
CHAD
SUDAN

L I B Y A

Tripolitania
Cyrenaica
Fezzan
Hamada el Homra

Libyan Desert
Plateau

Nubian Desert

Cairo
Alexandria
Tripoli
Benghazi
Aswân
L. Nasser

Oasis of Siwa
Oasis of Farâfra
Oasis of Dakhla
Oasis of Kufra
Oasis of Jalo

Tropic of Cancer

Statute Miles
0   100   200   300

ISRAEL

MEDITERRANEAN SEA

Ashqelon
Gazal
Gaza
Rafah
El 'Arish
Qeseima
'Aqaba

34

PORT SAID (BÛR SAÎD)
Damietta
(Dimyât)
Rosetta
(Rashîd)
Baltim
Abu Qîr
ALEXANDRIA
(El Iskandarîya)
Burg el 'Arab
Arabs G.
El Hammam
El 'Alamein

Râs el Daba

Qattara
El Maghra
Depression

L i b y a n

D e s e r t

Bawîti

Statute Miles
20   40   60

El Harra

Sabkhet
Bardawîl

D e s e r t

32

El Manzala
Shirbîn
Mansûra
Damanhûr
Tanta
Benha
Zifta
El Mahalla
Samannûd
Farasdaq
El Mansûra
Ismailîya
El Salhîya
Tell el Kebîr
Abu Hammâd
Bilbeis
CAIRO (EL QAHIRA) Suez
Heliopolis
Matarîya
El Gîza
Pyramids
MEMPHIS
El Badrshein
El Atyâba
Birket Qârûn
El Faiyûm
Ihnâsya el Madîna
W. Meweïh
El Bahnasa
El Wâdi el Maghâgha
Abu Girg
Beni Mazâr
Samalût
El Fashn
El Hîba

Fuad
Qantara
El Shatt
Suez Canal
Fayid
Bitter Lakes
El Shatt
El Suwes
Tuafiq
Geb.
Ataqa
N. Galâla Plateau
S.
Galâla Plateau
Deir Mâr Pâulos

ISRAEL
MILITARY ADMINISTRATION

SINAI PENINSULA

Geb. el Tîh
Geb. Hilâl
Geb. el Igma
Nakhl
Ruqq
Feirân
G. Serbâl
Geb. Katherina
Monastery of St. Catherine
St. Musa

Gulf of Susuez

Deir Abu
Tînna
G. Umm Shomâr
Râs Gharib

E G Y P T

L O W E R

E G Y P T

Wadi el Natrûn
Deir Suriâni
Deir Makâr

Nile

Shibîn el Kom
Assiût
Helwân
Tûrah
Tâmiya
Shibîne
Sôl
Tâsta
Bush
Beni Suef

N i l e

© John Bartholomew & Son Ltd. Edinburgh

NORTH-WEST AFRICA

LIBYA

NIGER

TUNISIA

ALGERIA

MOROCCO

SPAIN

MEDITERRANEAN SEA

ATLANTIC OCEAN

SAHARA

MAURITANIA

SPANISH SAHARA

Canary Islands

Madeira (Port.)

Tropic of Cancer

Statute Miles

Seville
Malaga
Gibraltar (U.K.)
Tanger (Tangier)
Ceuta (Sp.)
Melilla

Casablanca
Rabat
Kénitra
Ksar el Kebir
Marrakech
El Jadida
Safi
Mogador
Agadir
Ifni
Tarfaya

Fès
Meknès
Oujda
Tlemcen
Oran
Mostaganem
Algiers
Bougie
Bône (Annaba)
Bizerte
Tunis
C. Bon
Sfax

Gafsa
Tozeur
Gabès
Médenine
Zuwārah
Nālūt
Ghudāmis (Ghadames)
Ghāt (Gat)

Tébessa
Biskra
Touggourt
Ouargla
Ghardaïa
Fort Lallemand
Fort Flatters
Fort Polignac

Laghouat
Aïn Sefra
El Goléa
In Salah
Djanet
In Amenas

Béchar
Beni Abbès
Igli
Ksabi
Reggan

Hassi Messaoud
Edjelé
Bordj Omar Driss

Plateau du Tademaït
Aïn Salah
Mac Mahon
Tamanrasset
Ahaggar
Ahnet

Fort Laperrine
Adrar des Iforas

Tindouf
Sebkha de Hodouf
Taoudenni

Fdérik

La Calle
C. Blanc (Nazairte)
Shidda

Madeira
Funchal
Porto Santo

Lanzarote
Fuerteventura
Gran Canaria
Las Palmas
Tenerife
La Palma

El Aiún (Port.)
Seguía el Hamra
C. Bojador

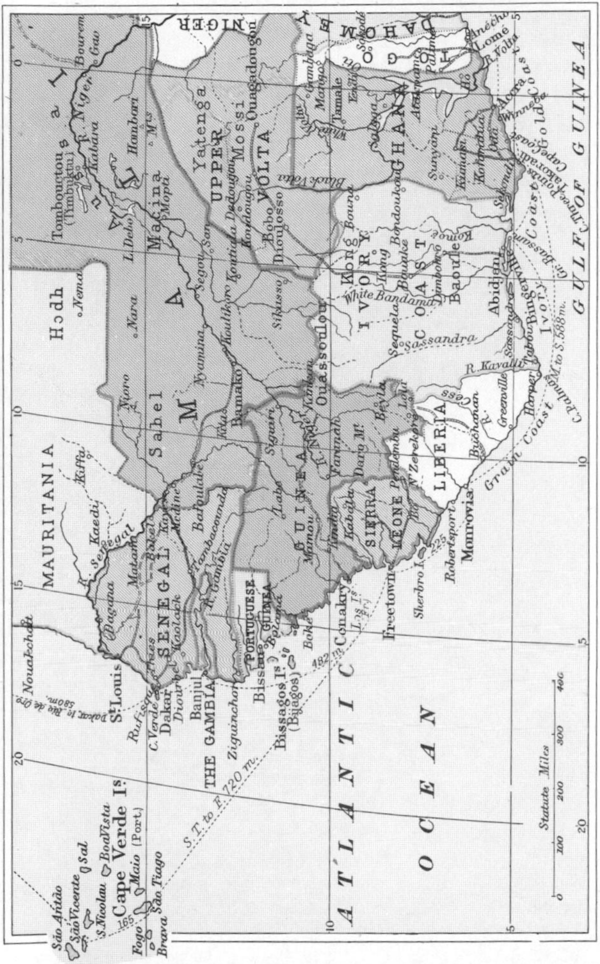
MAURITANIA
Hodh
Sahel
MALI
Macina
Yatenga
UPPER VOLTA
Mossi
NIGER
DAHOMEY
TOGO
GHANA
IVORY COAST
LIBERIA
SIERRA LEONE
GUINEA
PORTUGUESE GUINEA
SENEGAL
THE GAMBIA
Cape Verde Is. (Port.)
São Antão
São Vicente
Sal
S. Nicolau
Boa Vista
Maio
São Tiago
Fogo
Brava
ATLANTIC OCEAN
GULF OF GUINEA
Gold Coast
Ivory Coast
Grain Coast
Tombouctou (Timbuktu)
R. Niger
Kabara
Bourem
Gao
Mopti
L. Debo
Segou
Bamako
Koulikoro
Nyamina
Nioro
Nara
Nema
Kiffa
Kaedi
R. Senegal
St. Louis
Nouakchott
Dakar
C. Verde
Rufisque
Thies
Kaolack
Diourbel
Matam
Bakel
Kayes
Medine
Bafoulabe
Tambacounda
R. Gambia
Banjul
Ziguinchor
Bissau
Bolama
Bissagos Is. (Bijagos)
Boke
Conakry
Los Is.
Freetown
Sherbro I.
Robertsport
Monrovia
Buchanan
Greenville
Harper
C. Palmas
R. Kavalli
R. Cess
Tabou
Sassandra
Abidjan
Bingerville
Gr. Bassam
Kong
Bouake
Bondoukou
Baoule
Dimbokro
Sequela
White Bandama
Komoe
Ouagadougou
Koudougou
Dedougou
Bobo Dioulasso
Koutiala
Sikasso
Ouassoulou
Kankan
Siguiri
Kouroussa
Faranah
Labe
Mamou
Kindia
Kabala
Beyla
Pendembu
N'Zerekore
Lola
Dabola
Tamale
Yendi
Gambaga
Mango
Salaga
Sunyani
Kumasi
Koforidua
Atakpame
Palime
Ho
Lomé
R. Volta
Anécho
Accra
Winneba
Sekondi
Takoradi
Cape Coast
Three Points
Black Volta
White Volta
Oti
Statute Miles
0 100 200 300 400
S.T. to F. 720 m.
Dakar to Rio de Oro 580 m.
482 m.
225
165
C. Palmas to S. 588 m.

Baiyuda
Desert
R. Nile
6th Cataract
Berber
El Damer
R. Atbara
Shendi
Tokar
RED
SEA
Ras Kasar
Farasan I.
Jizan
Yemen

Omdurman
Khartoum
Khashm
el Gerba
Goz Regeb
Kereri
Suakin
Agordat
Kassala
Keren
Massawa
Farasan I.
Kamarun
Al Hudaydeh
DEM. REP.
OF YEMEN

Wad Medani
El Dueim
Sennar
Singa
Jebel Mosul
R. Dinder
R. Rahad
Roseires
Galabat
Gondar
Er
Tigrai
Adowa
Ras Dashan
15,158
Debra Tabor
Guna
Asmara
Mocha
Perim I.
Assab
Shugra
Aden
Bab el Mandeb
Obock
Zeila
G. of Aden

SUDAN
Kosti
R. White Nile
Renk
Malakal
Taufikia
Nasir
R. Sobat
Kodok
L. Tana
Abbai (Blue Nile)
Gojjam
Dessye
Magdala
Debra Markos
Ankober
Addis Ababa
Shoa
Diredawa
Harar
FR. TER.
OF AFARS
& ISSAS
Djibouti
Dikhil
SOMALIA
Berbera
Hargeisa
Bohotleh
Damot

Shambe
Bor
Mongalla
Rejaf
Torit
Folo Ilat
Lamule
Kitgum
Moroto
Muhisima
Gulu
UGANDA
L. Kioga
Soroti
Mbale
Mt. Elgon
14,176
Tororo
R. Baro
R. Sobat
Gambeila
Jimma
Shegada
Kafa
R. (Omo)
Bako
ETHIOPIA
(ABYSSINIA)
L. Abaya
Negelli
L. Stefanie
Moyale
Lake
Rudolf
Webbi Shebeli
Imi
Warandab
Walwal
Gerloqubi
Didiga
Dawa
Lugh Ferrandi
Ogaden

SOMALI REP.
Bardera
Wajir
R. Juba
Webbe Scebeli
Mogadishu
(Mogadiscio)
Merca
Brava
Benadir Coast

RWANDA
BURUNDI
L. Albert
R. Semliki
Bunyoro
Mubende
Entebbe
Kampala
Jinja
L. Victoria
Bukoba
L. Edward
Lake
Kivu
Shinyanga
Mwanza
Kahama
L. Eyasi
Singida
Tabora
Kondoa
TANZANIA
Kilimatinde
Dodoma
Rungwa
Kilosa
Morogoro

KENYA
Nanyuki
Mt. Kenya
Nyeri
Fort Hall
Nakuru
Eldama
Nairobi
Kitui
Machakos
Embu
Lorian Swamp
Garissa
Equator
Chisimaio
(Kismayu)

L. Baringo
L. Naivasha
L. Natron
Kilimanjaro
19,340
Moshi
Arusha
Manyara
Korogwe
Pangani
Bagamoyo
Zanzibar
Dar es Salâam
Kibwezi
Voi
Bura
Lamu
Witu
Malindi
Kilindini
Mombasa
Tanga
Pemba I.
Sa'dani

INDIAN
OCEAN
Mombasa to Bombay 2510 m.
Zanzibar to Aden 1000 m.

Statute Miles
100 200

© John Bartholomew & Son Ltd. Edinburgh

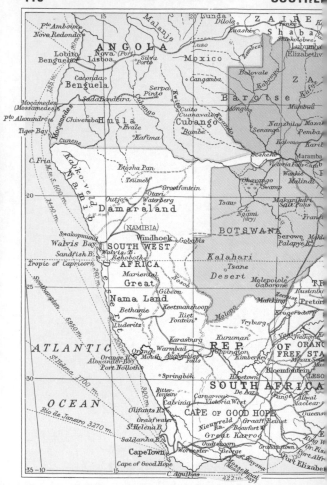

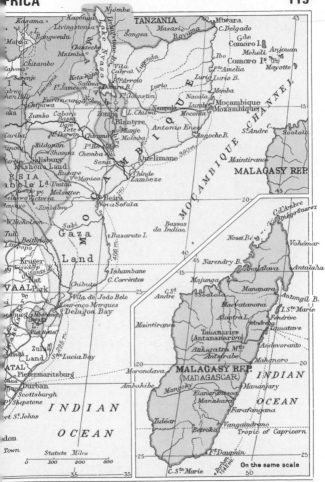

TANZANIA

Njombe

Kasama
L. Bangweulu
Livingstonia
Mzimba
Chisecha
Kaporoga
Songea
Masasi
Ruvuma
Mtwara
C. Delgado

Mare
Chitambo
Senje
Chipawa
Kota-Kota
Salima
Domira B.
Ft. Jameson
Furancungo
Vila Cabral
Ft. Johnston
Lugenda
P.to Arrolo
Ft. Amelia
Lurio
Lurio B.
Meiuba
Nacala
Lumbo
Moçambique
Mozambique
Ibo
Comoro I.
Gde
Comoro I.
Moheli
Anjouan
Mayotte
S.to Andre
Soalala

Zumbo
Cabora
Bassa
Dam
Tete
Mt. Darwin
Charoma
Shamva
Chemba
Sena
Zomba
L. Chilwa
Blantyre
Mianje
Moluba
P.to Herald
Chinde
Zambeze
Antonio Enes
Angoche B.
Nampula
Mecouta
390m.
Chelimane
Maintirano
MALAGASY REP.

Kariba
Sinoia
Salisbury
Mashona Land
Rusape
Manica
Melsetter
Beira
Nova Sofala
Umtali
Victoria
Zimbabwe

W. Nicholson
Tuli
Beitbridge
Limpopo
Sabi
Bazaruto I.
Bassas
da Indias
Cd'Ambre
Diego Suarez
Nossi Bé
Vohémar

Gaza
Land
Inhambane
C. Corrèntes
Narendry B.
Analalava
Antalaha

Kruger
Nat.
Park
Chibuto
Vila de João Belo
Lourenço Marques
Delagoa Bay
Majunga
Soalala
Maevatanana
Alaotra L.
Andevoranto
Antongil B.
I. S.te Marie
Mananara

VAAL
Zulu
Land
S.ta Lucia Bay
Maintirano
Morondava
Ambohibe
Mangoky
Tananarive
(Antananarivo)
Ankaratra M.ts
Antsirabe
Andevoranto
Tamatave

Pietermaritzburg
Durban
Scottsburgh
P. Skepstone
t St. Johns
MALAGASY REP.
(MADAGASCAR)
Fianarangsoa
Manakara
Mananjary
Farafangana

INDIAN
OCEAN
INDIAN
OCEAN
Tuléar
Betroka
Vangaindrano
Tropic of Capricorn

Town
don

Statute Miles
0   100   200   300

On the same scale

Ft. Dauphin
C. S.te Marie

© – John Bartholomew & Son.Ltd.,Edinburgh

Statute Miles

0   500   1000

Equator

Gilbert (UK) Is.

Admiralty Is.
Manus
New Hanover
Bismarck Archipelago
Madang
Rabaul
Lae
Huon G.
Mt Victoria
NEW GUINEA
G. of Papua
Moresby
York
Samarai
China Str.
Louisiade Arch.

New Ireland
Lokopo
New Britain

Bougainville
Solomon
Choiseul
Islands
New Georgia
Isabel
Guadalcanal
Malaita
San Cristobal
Rennell

Sta Cruz Is. (UK)
Ndeni

CORAL SEA

Great Barrier Reef
Cairns
Willis Is.
Halifax B.
Townsville
Port Denison
Chesterfield Is. (Fr.)
Mackay

Espiritu Santo
Banks Is.
Malekula
New Hebrides (UK & Fr.)
Efate
Eromanga

Fiji Is.

PACIFIC

Rockhampton
Hervey B.
Bundaberg
Fraser or
Maryborough
Gt Sandy I.
Gympie
Toowoomba
Moreton Bay
Ipswich
Brisbane
C. Byron
Grafton

New Caledonia (Fr.)
Noumea
Loyalty Is.

Tropic of Capricorn

OCEAN

ISLAND
A
SOUTH WALES
Tamworth
Port Macquarie
Maitland
Bathurst
Newcastle
Katoomba
Goulburn
Wollongong
Sydney
Canberra
Mt Kosciusko
Mt Townsend
Cape Howe
ORIA
Melbourne
Wilsons Prom.
Bass Strait
Launceston
bart

Norfolk I. (Aust.)

Lord Howe I. (Aust.)

Kermadec Is. (NZ)

TASMAN

SEA

NEW
ZEALAND

North C.
Hamilton
New Plymouth
Auckland
East C.
Gisborne
Mt Egmont
Cook Str.
Napier
Mt Ruapehu
Nelson
Wellington
Hokitika
South I.
West C.
Mt Cook 3764
Christchurch
Chatham
Dunedin
Stewart I.
Invercargill

© — John Bartholomew & Son, Ltd. Edinburgh

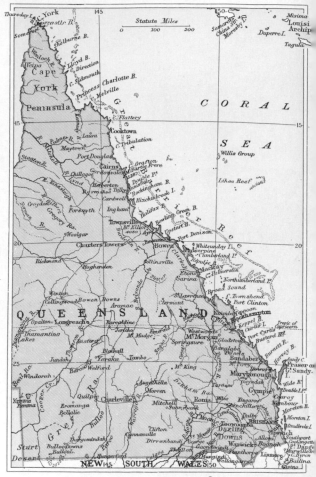

Statute Miles

0   100   200

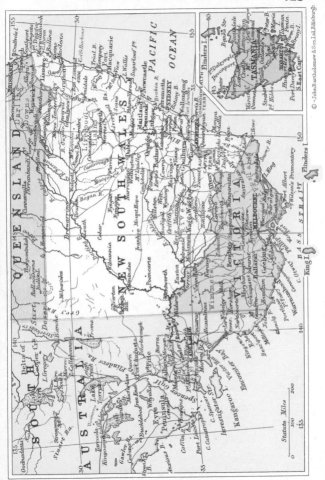

© John Bartholomew & Son Ltd.Edinburgh

Statute Miles
0   100   200   300

C. Lévêque
Black
Rocks
Dampier
Land
Derby
Roebuck B.
Broome
La Grange B.
C. Bossut
Eighty Mile Beach

Great Sandy
Desert

Turtle I.
Port Hedland
Mt Goldsworthy
Le Grey R.
Pilbarra
Goldfield
Marble Bar
Nullagine

Dampier Archipelago
Monte Bello Is.
Barrow I.
Preston
King Bay
West Pilbarra Goldfield
Forrest R.
Wittenoom
Nth West C.
Exmouth G.
Onslow
Deepdale
Mt Tom Price
Mt Bruce
4,024
Rudall
Separation Well

Pt Cloates
Yanrey
Ashburton R.
Mt Ashburton
Goldfield
Mt
Whaleback
Tropic of Capricorn
Disappointment
Gibson
Desert

C. Farquhar
Barlee R.
Gascoyne R.
Fortescue R.
WESTERN
C. Cuvier
Geographe Channel
Carnarvon
Bernier I.
Dorre I.
Shark
Bay
Naturaliste Chan.
Kennedy
Rd.
Lyons R.
Mt Augustus
Mt Labouchere
L. Carnegie

Dirk Hartog I.
Perth R.
Hamelin
Pool
Steep Pt.
Gascoyne R.
Mt Nairn
Murchison R.
L. Wells

Gantheaume B.
Murchison R.
Ajana
Northampton
Houtman Rocks
or Abrolhos
Geraldton
Dongora
Mingenew
AUSTRALIA
Mt Murchison
Nannine
Meekatharra
Wiluna
L. Carnegie
Nicholson
Rd.
Murchison Goldfield
Austin
1,400
East Murchison
Goldfield
L. Throssell
L. Yeo

Yalgoo
Mt Magnet
Sandstone
L. Rason

Mullewa Goldfield
L. Barlee
Leonora
Morgans
Laverton
L. Raeside

Mt Monger
North Coolgardie
Goldfield
Niagara (Dry & Salt)
Moora
L. Moore
Menzies

Kalannie
Miling
Mt Jackson
Kanowna
North East
Coolgardie
Goldfield
Bullfinch
Kalgoorlie
Benbubbin
Yilgarn
Boulder
Bardoc
Coolgardie

Dowerin
Southern Cross
Goldfield
L. Lefroy
Temby
Merredin
Goldfield
Northam
York
Beverley
L. Cowan
Norseman

PERTH
Fremantle
Mandurah
Warong
Narrogin
Dundas
Newdegate
Dundas Goldfield
Salmon
Gums
Russell Rd.

C. Naturaliste
Geographe B.
Bunbury
Busselton
Collie
Wagin
Ravensthorpe
Ravensthorpe
Hills
Hopetoun
Doubtful I. Bay
Esperance
C. Pasley
Recherche Arch.

Augusta
C. Leeuwin
Flinders B.
Blackwood R.
Katanning
Frankland R.
Tambellup
Cranbrook
Stirling
Ra.
Mt Barker
Mt Knob
Denmark
Nornalup Inlet
Albany
King George Sd.

115
120
20
25
30
35

I N D I A N   O C E A N

© – John Bartholomew & Son, Ltd. Edinburgh

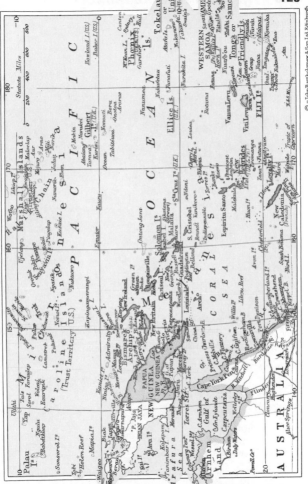

Statute Miles

0 200 400 600 800

PACIFIC OCEAN

Palau Is.

Caroline Islands (Trust Territory) (U.S.)

Marshall Islands

Gilbert Is. (U.K.)

Ellice Is. (U.K.)

Phoenix Is.

Tokelau or Union Is.

WESTERN SAMOA

AMERICAN SAMOA

FIJI IS.

New Caledonia

CORAL SEA

Solomon Is.

New Britain

Bismarck Archip.

NEW GUINEA

PAPUA

IRIAN JAYA

CORAL SEA

New Hebrides

Tonga or Friendly Is.

AUSTRALIA

Gulf of Carpentaria

Arnhem Land

Cape York Pen.

Torres Str.

Arafura Sea

Tropic of Capricorn

Statute Miles

Divisions coloured
are statistical areas

Statute Miles

Divisions coloured
are statistical areas

© –John Bartholomew & Son,Ltd.Edinburgh

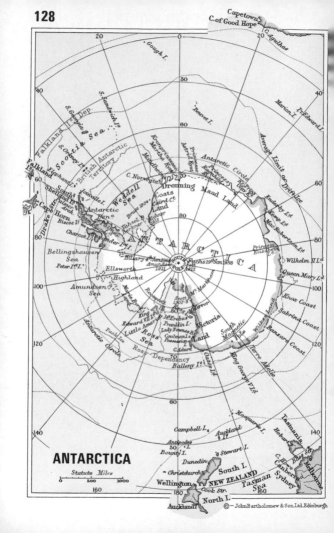

ANTARCTICA

Statute Miles

0   500   1000

© — John Bartholomew & Son, Ltd. Edinburgh.

Gazetteer

Entries include page number references as divided into **a, b, c** and **d** thus:

Aberdeen, city and port, N.E. Scotland 62b

Abidjan, port and cap. of Ivory Coast, Africa 115b

Accra, cap. of Ghana, West Africa 115b

Aconcagua, highest peak of Andes; 23,035 ft. 52a

Acre, state, Brazil 50a

Addis Ababa, cap. of Ethiopia 117b

Adelaide, cap. of South Australia 123d

Afghanistan, an independent state on the N.W. frontier of Pakistan; cap. Kabul 107b

Ahmadabad, town and cap. of Gujarat, India 102b

Akron, city, Ohio, S. of Cleveland 26d

Al Bayda', town, Libya 112c

Alabama, state, U.S.A.; cap. Montgomery 28d

Alagoas, state, Brazil 51b

Alaska, state of U.S.A., in N.W. America 42a

Albania, rep., on the Balkan Peninsula; cap. Tiranë 83c

Albany, city and cap. of New York 24b

Alberta, prov., Canada; cap. Edmonton 14a

Albuquerque, town, New Mexico 31c

Alexandria, city and port, U.A.R. 113c

Algeria, rep., on north coast of Africa 114a

Algiers (Alger), cap. of Algeria 114a

Allentown, city, Pennsylvania, N.W. of Philadelphia 25c

Alma Ata, town, Kazak, N.E. of Frunze 90b

Amapá, state, Brazil 48b

Amarillo, town, Texas 31c

Amazon, river, S. America, 4,000 m. long 46b

Amazonas, state, Brazil 50a

American Samoa, prov., Pacific Ocean 125b
Amman, cap. of Jordan 106a
Amsterdam, cap. and port, Netherlands 70b
Amur, river, U.S.S.R., enters Sea of Okhotsk 91b
Andhra Pradesh, state, India 102d
Andorra, republic, Pyrenees Mts. 75b
Andros Island, Bahamas, W. Indies 44a
Angola, Portuguese col., W. Africa; cap. Luanda 111c
Anguilla, island, Leeward Is., W. Indies 45a
Anhwei, prov., China 97a
Ankara, cap. of Turkey, S.E. of Istanbul 108c
Annapurna, mt. Nepal, 26,504 ft. 104a
Antigua I., Leeward Is., W. Indies 45a
Arab Rep. of Egypt (A.R.E.), Africa; cap. Cairo 112a
Ararat, Mount, Turkey, 16,946 ft. 108a
Argentina, rep., S. America; cap. Buenos Aires 47c
Arizona, state, W. U.S.A.; cap. Phoenix 39a
Arkansas, state, S. U.S.A.; cap. Little Rock 31a
Armenia, rep., U.S.S.R.; cap. Yerevan 89b
Ascension Island, S. Atlantic Ocean 111c
Assam, state, India; cap. Shillong 103a
Asuncion, port and cap. of Paraguay 50d
Athens (Athínai), city and cap. of Greece 85d
Atlanta, cap. of Georgia, U.S.A. 28d
Auckland, prov. and city, North I., N.Z. 126a
Austin, cap. of Texas, on Colorado River 31d
Australia, state, cap. Canberra, smallest continent 121c
Austria, rep., Cent. Europe; cap. Vienna 80b
Azerbaijan, rep., U.S.S.R.; cap. Baku 89b
Badrinath, mt., India/Tibet; 23,190 ft. 104c
Baghdad, city and cap. of Iraq 106b
Bahama Islands, Brit., group, W. Indies 45c
Bahia, state, Brazil 51b

Bahrain, island and state, The Gulf 107c
Baikal, Lake, U.S.S.R.; area 13,500 sq. m. 91c
Baku, port and cap. of Azerbaijan 89b
Balearic Isles, group, in Mediterranean 75d
Balkhash, Lake, Kazak, U.S.S.R. 90b
Baltimore, city and port, Maryland 25d
Bamako, cap of Mali, on R. Niger 115a
Bandar Seri Begawan, town and cap. of Brunei 99c
Bandarpunch, mt., India 104c
Bangalore, town and cap. of Karnataka, India 102d
Bangkok see Krung Thep
Bangui, town, cap. of Cent. Afr. Rep. 111a
Banjul, cap. of The Gambia, W. Africa 115c
Barbados, island, W. Indies 45b
Barbuda, island, Leeward Is., W. Indies 45a
Barcelona, city and port, Spain 75b
Basildon, new town, Essex, England 61d
Bata, town and cap. of Equat. Guinea 116d
Baton Rouge, city, cap. of Louisiana 37c
Bear Lake, Great, N.-W. Terr., Canada 12b
Beaumont, town, Texas, S.E. of Dallas 36d
Beirût, city and cap. of Lebanon 109a
Belfast, city port and cap. of N. Ireland 64a
Belgium, kingdom, W. Europe; cap. Brussels 71c
Belgrade = Beograd
Belize, state, Cent. Amer., cap. Belmopan 44b
Belmopan, cap. of Belize (B. Honduras) 44b
Belo Horizonte, city, Brazil, N. of Rio de Janeiro 51c
Benghazi, port, Libya, N. Africa 112c
Benoni, town, S. Africa 118d
Beograd (Belgrade), city, cap. of Yugoslavia 83a
Berkeley, city, California, on San Francisco B. 40d
Berlin, city, Germany, on R. Spree 78b

Bermuda, island group, N. Atlantic 11a
Berne (Bern), cap. of Switzerland 76c
Bhutan, state in the Himalayas 103a
Bihar, state, India; cap. Patna 103a
Birkenhead, port, Merseyside, England 60b
Birmingham, city, Alabama 28d
Birmingham, city, Warwicks, England 60b
Blackburn, town, Lancs, England 59d
Blackpool, seaside town, Lancs., England, 59d
Bloemfontein, cap. of O.F.S., S. Africa 118d
Bogotá, cap. of Colombia, S. America 48c
Bolivia, rep., S. America; cap. Sucre 50c
Bolton, town, Greater Manchester, England 59d
Bombay, city and port, W. India, cap. of Maharashtra 102d
Bonn, city and cap. of W. Germany 77a
Bordeaux, city and port, S.W. France 72d
Boston, city and port, cap. of Mass., U.S.A. 24b
Botswana, rep., S. Africa, cap. Gaborone 118d
Bournemouth, town, Dorset, England 60d
Bradford, city, W. Yorks, England 59b
Brahmaputra, river, Asia, flows into Bay of Bengal,
    1800 m. long 103a
Brasília, federal capital of Brazil 51a
Brazil, rep., S. America; cap. Brasília 46b
Brazzaville, town, cap. of People's Rep. of the Congo,
    Central Africa 116d
Bremen, city, W. Germany 78a
Bridgetown, cap. of Barbados 45b
Bridgeport, city, Long Island Sd., Conn. 25a
Brighton, seaside tn., E. Sussex, England 61c
Brisbane, port and cap. of Queensland 122d
Bristol, city and port, Avon, Eng. 60d
British Columbia, prov., W. Canada 14c

British Solomon Is., group, Pacific Oc. 125d
Brunei, state, N.W. Borneo 99c
Brussels (Bruxelles), cap. of Belgium 71c
Bucuresti (Bucharest), city, cap. of Romania 83b
Budapest, city and cap. of Hungary 81a
Buenos Aires, fed. cap. of Argentina 52b
Buffalo, city, New York, on Lake Erie 26a
Bujumbura, town, cap. of Burundi 111a
Bulawayo, town, S. Rhodesia 119a
Bulgaria, rep., Balkan Pen.; cap. Sofia 83a
Burma, rep., E. of India; cap. Rangoon 98a
Burundi, rep., central Africa 111a
Byelorussia, rep., U.S.S.R., cap. Minsk. 87c
Caicos Islands, W. Indies, N. of Hispaniola 45c
Cairo, cap. of A.R.E., on the Nile 112a
Calcutta, city, port and cap. of W. Bengal 103a
Calgary, city, Alberta, S. of Edmonton 14b
California, state, W. U.S.A.; cap. Sacramento 39c
Cambodia, Khmer Republic 98d
Cambridge, co. town, Cambs., England 61a
Cambridge, city, Mass., suburb of Boston 24b
Camden, city, New Jersey, on Delaware River 25d
Cameroun, republic, Central Africa, cap. Yaoundé 116b
Canada, state, N. America, cap. Ottawa 12 & 13
Canary Islands, Span. group, off N.W. Africa 114d
Canberra, fed. cap. of Australia 123b
Canton, town, Ohio 26d
Cape of Good Hope (Cape Province), prov. of
    Republic of South Africa 118d
Cape Town, port and cap. of Cape Prov. 118c
Cape Verde Islands, group, Atlantic Oc., off N.W. Africa 115c
Caracas, cap. of Venezuela 48c
Cardiff, city and cap. of Wales 60d

Columbus, cap. of Ohio, U.S.A. 27c
Columbus, town, Georgia 28d
Comoro Islands, Moçambique Channel 119b
Conakry, port and cap. of Guinea, W. Africa 115d
Congo, river, central Africa, flows 3000 m. to Atlantic Oc. 111a
Congo, Dem. Rep. of, see Zaire
Congo, People's Rep. of, W. Africa; cap. Brazzaville 116d
Connecticut, state, N.E. U.S.A.; cap. Hartford 25a
Cook Islands, Polynesia, Pacific Ocean 53b
Cook, Mt., N.Z. 127a
Copenhagen (København), cap. of Denmark 69d
Cork, city and co., Rep. of Ireland 65d
Corpus Christi, town, Texas 31d
Costa Rica, republic, Central America, cap. San José 44b
Cotapaxi, mt., Ecuador; 19,344 ft. 49a
Coventry, city, Warwicks, England 61a
Cuba, island and rep., West Indies, cap. Havana 45c
Cyprus, island and rep., E. Mediterranean, cap. Nicosia 108d
Czechoslovakia, rep., central Europe, cap. Prague 80b
Dacca, city, E. Bengal, cap. of Bangladesh 103a
Dahomey, rep., W. Africa; cap. Porto Novo 116a
Dakar, port and cap., Senegal, West Africa 115c
Dallas, city, Texas, E. of Fort Worth 31c
Damascus, city and cap. of Syria 109b
Damavand, mt., Iran, 18,934 ft. 107a
Danube, river of Cent. Europe, length 1740 m. 80b
Dar es Salaam, port, and cap., Tanzania 117d
Dayton, city, Ohio, W.S.W. of Columbus 27c
Dearborn, town, Michigan 26c
Delaware, river rises in New York and flows to
    Delaware B. 25c
Delaware, Atlantic state, U.S.A.; cap. Dover 25d
Delhi, city and cap. of India 102b

Denmark, kingdom, Europe; cap. Copenhagen 69d
Denver, cap. of Colorado, U.S.A. 39a
Derby, co. town, Derbyshire, England 61a
Descabezado, mt., Chile 52c
Des Moines, city and cap. of Iowa 32c
Detroit, city and port, Michigan 26c
Dykh Tau, mt., U.S.S.R. 89c
Djakarta, see Jakarta
Dnepropetrovsk, town, Ukraine, S.W of Kharkov 88c
Dominica, island, Leeward Is., W. Indies 45b
Dominican Rep. (Santo Domingo), Hispaniola West
    Indies, cap. Santo Domingo 45a
Donetsk, town, Ukraine, S.E. of Kharkov 88b
Dortmund, city, W. Germany, N.E. of Cologne 77a
Dresden, city, E. Germany, E.S.E. of Leipzig 78b
Dublin, city, port, county and cap. of Rep. of Ireland 65a
Dudley, town, W. Midlands, England 60b
Duluth, city and lake port, Minnesota 30a
Dundee, cy. & pt., E. Region, Scot., on R. Tay 63a
Dunedin, city, South I., New Zealand 127d
Durban, port, Natal, on Indian Ocean 119c
Düsseldorf, city, W. Germany, on the Rhine 77a
East London, port, Cape Province 118d
Ecuador, rep., S. America 49a
Edinburgh, cap. of Scotland, on Firth of Forth 63a
Edmonton, cap. of Alberta, Canada 14b
Elbrus, highest peak, Caucasus, U.S.S.R. 89c
Elizabeth, city, New Jersey, W. of Brooklyn 25c
Ellice Islands, British group in the Pacific, N. of Fiji 125b
El Paso, city, Texas, on Rio Grande 31c
El Salvador, rep., Cent. Amer., cap. San Salvador 44b
England, kingdom, with Wales forms the S. portion of
    Great Britain 58d

Equatorial Guinea, state, W. Africa 116d
Erie, Lake, between Ontario and U.S.A. 16d
Erie, town, Pennsylvania 26b
Espírito Santo, state, Brazil 51d
Essen, town, W. Germany 77a
Estonia, rep., U.S.S.R.; cap. Tallinn 86d
Ethiopia (Abyssinia), kingdom, E. Africa, cap. Addis
    Ababa 117b
Etna, Mount, volcano, Sicily, 10,741 feet 82d
Euphrates, river, W. Asia, flows 1700 m. to The Gulf 106b
Evansville, town, Indiana, on Ohio river 35b
Everest, mt. peak, Himalayas, highest in the world,
    29,028 ft. 104a
F.T.A.I. = French Territory of the Afars and the Issas 117b
Faerøerne, Dan. islands in N. Atlantic Oc. 56b
Falkland Islands Dependency, Brit. col., S. Atlantic 52d
Fernando de Noronha, state, Brazil 46b
Fernando Póo, isl., Equat. Guinea, W. Africa 116a
Fès, town, Morocco, E. of Rabat 114c
Fiji Islands, state, in Pacific Ocean 125b
Finland, republic, Europe; cap. Helsinki 67a
Finsteraarhorn, Switzerland, Bernese Alps 76d
Flint, town, Michigan 26c
Florida, a S. Atlantic state, U.S.A.; cap. Tallahassee 28d
Fort Lamy, tn. and cap. of Chad, Africa 116b
Fort Wayne, city, Indiana, S.E. of Chicago 33d
Fort Worth, city, Texas, W. of Dallas 36a
France, republic, W. Europe; cap. Paris 73a
Frankfurt-am-Main, city, W. Germany 77b
Freetown, cap. of Sierra Leone, Africa 115d
French Guiana, prov., S. America 48a
French Terr. of the Afars and the Issas (F.T.A.I.); cap.
    Djibouti 117b

Fresno, town, California 41a
Fuji-san, mt., Japan, S.W. of Tokio, 12,388 ft. 96a
Fukien, province, China 97b
Gaborone, cap. of Botswana 118d
Gabon, rep., Cent. Africa; cap. Librevelle 116d
Gambia, the river and rep., W. Africa; cap. Banjul 115c
Ganga, river, India, flows 1,500 miles into B. of Bengal 103a
Ganges = Ganga 103a
Gangtok, town and cap. of Sikkim 103a
Gary, town, Indiana 33c
Gateshead, town, Durham, opp. Newcastle upon Tyne 59a
Geelong, city, Victoria, S. of Bendigo 123d
Genova, city and port, N.W. Italy, on G. of Genoa 82a
Georgetown, cap. of Guyana 48a
Georgia, S. Atlantic state, U.S.A.; cap. Atlanta 28d
Georgia, republic, U.S.S.R.; cap. Tbilisi 89b
Germany, E., rep., Europe 78b
Germany, W., rep., Europe 78a
Germiston, town, S. Africa 118d
Ghana, rep., W. Africa; cap. Accra 115b
Gibraltar, Br. fortress and town, S. Spain 74d
Gilbert Islands, British group, Pacific Ocean 125a
Glasgow, city and port, Scotland, on the Clyde 63a
Glendale, town, California 41b
Goiás, state, Brazil 51a
Gorkiy (Nizhni Novgorod), city, U.S.S.R., E. of Moscow 86b
Göteborg, port, Sweden, on Gota river 67d
Grand Rapids, city, Michigan, N.W. of Detroit 33b
Grays Thurrock, town, Essex, England 61d
Great Salt Lake, Utah, U.S.A. 38b
Greece, kingdom, S.E. Europe; cap. Athens 85d
Greenland, Danish island, N. America 54b
Greensboro, town, N. Carolina 29a

Grenada, island, W. Indies, Windward Is. 45b
Guadalajara, city, Mexico 44c
Guadeloupe, island, Leeward Is., W. Indies 45b
Guam, island, Marianas Is., Pacific Ocean 53c
Guanabara, state, Brazil 51c
Guatemala, rep., central America 44b
Guatemala City, cap. of Guatemala 44b
Guinea, rep., W. Africa; cap. Conakry 115d
Gujarat, state, W. India; cap. Ahmadabad 102b
Guyana, rep., S. America; cap. Georgetown 48a
Hague, The ('s-Gravenhage), cy., seat of govt.,
    Netherlands 70d
Haiti, rep., Hispaniola, W. Indies; cap. Port-au-Prince 45c
Halifax, port and cap. of Nova Scotia 19d
Hamburg, city and port, W. Germany, on Elbe 78b
Hamilton, city, Ontario, S.W. of Toronto 16d
Hammond, town, Indiana 33c
Hannover, town, W. Germany 78b
Hanoi, cy. and cap. of N. Vietnam 98b
Harbin, town, N.E. China, on Sungari river 95a
Hartford, town, Connecticut 25a
Haryana, state, N. India 104c
Havana, port and cap. of Cuba, W. Indies 45c
Hawaii, largest of the Hawaiian Islands and state,
    U.S.A.; cap. Honolulu 43b
Heilungkiang, prov., China 95a
Helsinki, port and cap. of Finland 67a
Himachal Pradesh, state, N. India 102b
Hobart, city and cap. of Tasmania 123b
Honan, prov., Central China 97c
Honduras, Brit., col., Cent. America; cap. Belmopan 44b
Hong Kong, British Island and col., S. China 95c
Honolulu, cap. of Hawaii, on Oahu Is. 43c

Hopeh, prov., China 95a
Houston, town and port, Texas, U.S.A. 36c
Huddersfield, town, Yorks., England 59b
Hull, port, Humberside, England, on the Humber 59b
Hunan, prov., China 97d
Hungary, rep., Cent. Europe; cap. Budapest 81a
Hupeh, prov., China 97c
Huron, Lake, bet. Canada and United States 16a
Hwang Ho, river, China, enters G. of Pohai 95c
Hyderabad, town, Andhra Pradesh, India 102d
Iceland, rep., N.W. Europe; cap. Reykjavik 56a
Idaho, W. state of U.S.A.; cap. Boise 38d
Illampu, mt., Bolivia; 21,490 ft. 50a
Illimani, mt., Bolivia; 22,579 ft. 50c
Illinois, N. cent. state, U.S.A.; cap. Springfield 32d
India, rep., S. Asia; cap. Delhi 102b
Indiana, N. central state of U.S.A. 22d
Indianapolis, city and cap. of Indiana 35b
Indonesia, rep., E. Indies; cap. Jakarta 99d
Indus, river, Pakistan, flows to Arabian Sea 102a
Inner Mongolia, aut. reg., China 95a
Iowa, N. cent. state, U.S.A.; cap. Des Moines 30b
Ipswich, co. town of Suffolk, England 61b
Iran (Persia), kingdom, W. Asia; cap. Tehran 107a
Iraq, rep., Asia; cap. Baghdad 106b
Ireland, island, W. of Great Britain, comprising Rep. of
   Ireland and N. Ireland 64 & 65
Islamabad, fed. cap. of Pakistan, N. of Rawalpindi 102b
Israel, rep., S.W. Asia 109c
Istanbul (Constantinople), city, Turkey 108c
Italy, rep., S. Europe; cap. Rome 82a
Ivory Coast, republic, W. Africa; cap. Abidjan 115b
Jackson, town and cap. of Mississippi 37b

Laos, kingdom, S.E. Asia; cap. Vientiane 98b
La Paz, city and dep., Bolivia, S. America 50c
La Plata, river, Argentina 52b
Latvia, rep., U.S.S.R.; cap. Riga 86d
Lebanon, state, W. Asia; cap. Beirut 109a
Leeds, city, W. Yorks, England 59b
Leeward Islands, Lesser Antilles, W. Indies 45a
Leicester, co. town of Leicestershire, England 61a
Leipzig, city, E. Germany, S.S.W. of Berlin 78b
Lena, river, U.S.S.R., flows to Arctic Ocean; 2,850 m.
    long 93a
Leningrad, city, U.S.S.R., near Lake Ladoga 86d
Lesotho (Basutoland), state, S. Africa 118d
Liaoning, prov., China 95a
Liberia, rep., West Africa; cap. Monrovia 115d
Libreville, tn. and cap. of Gabon, Cent. Africa 116d
Libya, rep., N. Africa; caps. Tripoli and Benghazi 112c
Liechtenstein, princ., E. Switz.; cap. Vaduz 76a
Lille, town, France, S.E. of Calais 73a
Lima, city and cap. of Peru 49c
Lincoln, town, cap. of Nebraska 30d
Lisbon (Lisboa), city, naval base and cap. of Portugal,
    on River Tagus 74c
Lithuania, rep., U.S.S.R.; chief town Vilnius 86d
Little Rock, cap. of Arkansas, U.S.A. 34c
Liverpool, city and port, Merseyside, England 59d
Llullaillaco, mt., Chile; 22,057 ft. 50c
Lódz, town, Poland, S.W. of Warsaw 79b
Logan, Mount, Yukon, N.W. Canada; 19,850 ft. 12a
Lomé, cap. of Togo, W. Africa 115b
London, cap. of England and U.K., on the Thames 61c
London, port of entry, Ontario, S.W. of Toronto 16d
Londonderry, co. and city, N. Ireland 64a

Malaysia, Peninsular, pt. fed., cap. Kuala Lumpur 100d
Maldive Islands, Indian Ocean, S.W. of Ceylon 92d
Mali, rep., cent. Africa; cap. Bamako 115a
Malta, island and state, in cent. Mediterranean; cap.
  Valletta 82d
Man, Isle of, Irish Sea; cap. Douglas 59d
Managua, town and cap. of Nicaragua 44b
Manchester, city, England 59b
Manila, port, Luzon I., Philippines 99c
Manitoba, prov., Canada; cap. Winnipeg 15d
Maranhão, state, Brazil 51a
Marseilles, port, France, S. coast 73c
Martinique, French island, W. Indies 45b
Maryland, Atlantic state of U.S.A.; cap. Annapolis 25d
Maseru City, cap. of Lesotho 118d
Massachusetts, state, U.S.A.; cap. Boston 24b
Mato Grosso, state, Brazil 50b
Matterhorn, alpine peak, Switzerland; 14,705 ft. 76d
Mauritius, state and I., Indian Ocean 3c
Mauritania, rep., W. Africa; cap. Nouakchott 115c
Meghalaya, state, N.E. India 103a
Mekong, river, S.E. Asia; length 2,750 miles 98b
Melbourne, cap. of Victoria, Australia 123b
Melilla, port and settlement, N. coast of Morocco 114a
Memphis, city, Tennessee, on Mississippi 28a
Mexico, state, N. America 44c
Mexico (City), cap. of the rep. of Mexico, N. America 44d
Miami, city and winter resort, Florida 29d
Michigan, state of U.S.A.; capital Lansing 22d
Michigan, Lake, N. America 22c
Milan, city, Lombardy, N. Italy 84c
Milwaukee, city and port, Wisconsin 33a
Minas Gerais, state, Brazil 51c

Nagaland, state of N.E. India 103b
Nagoya, town, Honshu I., Japan 96a
Naha, town and cap. of Ryukyu Is. 95d
Nairobi, cap. of Kenya, East Africa 117c
Namibia = South West Africa 118a
Nanda Devi, mt., Himalayas, Uttar Pradesh 104 c
Nanga Parbat, mt., Kashmir; 26,620 ft. 102b
Nanking (Nan-ch'ing), city, China, on the Yangtze Kiang 97a
Naples, city and naval base, Italy, S.E. of Rome 82d
Nashville, cap. of Tennessee, on Cumberland R. 35d
Nassau, cap. of Bahamas, New Providence I. 44a
Natal, prov., S. Africa; cap. Pietermaritzburg 119c
Nauru Island, Pacific, N.E. of Solomon Islands 125a
Nebraska, state, U.S.A.; cap. Lincoln 30d
Nepal, independent state, in the Himalayas 102 & 103
Netherlands, kingdom, W. Europe; caps. Amsterdam
    and The Hague 70d
Nevada, west. state, U.S.A.; cap. Carson City 39c
Nevis, I., Leeward Is., W. Indies 45a
Newark, city, New Jersey, N.W. of Staten I. 25c
New Bedford, town, Massachusetts 25a
New Brunswick, E. maritime prov. of Canada 19d
New Caledonia, French island, in S. Pacific 125b
Newcastle, port, New South Wales, N. of Sydney 123a
Newcastle upon Tyne, city and port, Tyne & Wear,
    England 59a
Newfoundland, island and prov. of E. Canada; cap. St
    John's 19a
New Guinea, island in W. Pacific 99b
New Hampshire, New England state, U.S.A.; cap.
    Concord 24b
New Haven, port, Connecticut, N.E. of N.Y. 25a
New Hebrides, island group, W. Pacific 125b

New Jersey, an Atlantic state of U.S.A.; cap.
  Trenton 25c
New Mexico, state, U.S.A.; cap. Santa Fe 39a
New Orleans, port of Louisiana 37d
Newport, tn. and port, Gwent, Wales 60d
Newport News, port, Virginia, N.W. of Norfolk 29b
New South Wales, state, Aust.; cap. Sydney 123b
New York, state, U.S.A.; cap. Albany 22a
New York, city and port, U.S.A. 25a
New Zealand, state, S. Pacific; cap. Wellington 126 & 127
Niagara Falls, city, New York, at falls of Niagara river 26a
Niamey, town and cap. of Niger, West Africa 116a
Nicaragua, rep., Cent. America; cap. Managua 44b
Nicaragua, Lake, S. America 44b
Nicosia, cap. of Cyprus, Mediterranean 108d
Niger, river, W. Africa, flows 2600 m. to G. of Guinea 110d
Niger, republic, W. Africa; cap. Niamey 110d
Nigeria, rep., West Africa; cap. Lagos 116a
Nile, river, N.E. Africa, flows 3600 miles to Mediterranean
  110b
Ningsia-Hui, aut. reg., China 94b
Niue, island, one of Cook Is. 53b
Norfolk, city, port and naval base, Virginia 29b
Norfolk Island, Pacific Oc., N.N.W. of N.Z. 121d
Northampton, co. town, Northants, England 61a
North Carolina, state, U.S.A.; cap. Raleigh 29b
North Dakota, a N. central state, U.S.A.; cap. Bismarck 30c
Northern Ireland, prov., U.K. 64a
Northern Territory, territory, Australia; cap. Darwin 120b
Northwest Territories, prov., Canada 12b
Norway, kingdom, Scandinavia, W. Europe; cap. Oslo 67c
Norwich, city, Norfolk, England 61b
Nottingham, city, co. town of Notts, England 61a

Nouakchott, cap. of Mauritania, W. Africa 115c
Nova Scotia, E. maritime prov., Canada; cap. Halifax 19d
Novosibirsk, town, on Ob river, U.S.S.R., E. of Omsk 90a
Nyasa, Lake, S.E. Africa 119a
Oakland, city, California, on San Francisco B. 40d
Ob, river, U.S.S.R., flows 2420 m. to Arctic Oc. 92b
Odessa, city and port, Ukraine, on Black Sea 88d
Ohio, state, U.S.A.; cap. Columbus 27c
Oklahoma, state, U.S.A. cap. Oklahoma City 31c
Oklahoma City, cap. of Oklahoma state, U.S.A. 31c
Oldham, town, Greater Manchester, England 59b
Omaha, city & riv. port, Nebraska, on Missouri 30b
Omsk, city, U.S.S.R., S.E. of Sverdlovsk 90a
Onega, Lake, U.S.S.R., E. of Lake Ladoga 86d
Ontario, E. province, Canada; cap. Toronto 17c
Ontario, Lake, between Canada and U.S.A. 17c
Oporto, city, Portugal, on the Douro 74a
Orange Free State, prov., S. Africa; cap. Bloemfontein 118d
Oregon, N.W. state of U.S.A.; cap. Salem 38d
Orissa, state, India; cap. Bhubaneswar 103c
Osaka, city and port, Honshu, Japan 96a
Oslo, city and cap. of Norway, on Oslo Fjord 67c
Ottawa, cap. of Canada, on Ottawa riv., Ontario 17b
Ouagadougou, town and cap. of Upper Volta 115a
Oxford, univ. and co. town of Oxfordshire, England 61a
Pakistan, state, S. Asia; cap. Islamabad 102b
Palermo, port and cap. of Sicily 82d
Panama City, port & cap. of the rep. of Panama 44b
Panama, republic, cent. America 44b
Papua, S.E. part of Papua, New Guinea; cap. Port
   Moresby 99b
Para, state, Brazil 51a
Paraguay, republic, S. America; cap. Asuncion 50d

Paraíba, state, Brazil 51b
Paramaribo, cap. of Surinam, S. America 48a
Paraná, state, Brazil 51c
Paraná, river, Brazil 51c
Paris, cap. of France, on the River Seine 73a
Pasadena, town, California 41b
Paterson, city, New Jersey, N.W. of New York 25c
Peking, city, Hopeh prov., cap. of China 95a
Pennsylvania, state, U.S.A., cap. Harrisburg 25c
Peoria, city, Illinois, S.W. of Chicago 32d
Perm, town, U.S.S.R., on river Kama 86b
Pernambuco, state, Brazil 51b
Perth, cap. of W. Australia, S.W. coast 124c
Peru, rep., S. America 49c
Philadelphia, city, Pennsyl., S.W. of New York 25c
Philippines, is. rep. E. Indies, cap. Manila 99c
Phnom Penh, cap. of Cambodia, Indo-China 98d
Phoenix, cap. of Arizona, N.W. of Tucson 39b
Phoenix Islands, group, N.E. of Fiji, Pacific Oc. 125a
Piaul, state, Brazil 51a
Pietermaritzburg, cap. of Natal, S. Africa 119c
Pitcairn Island, E. Pacific, S.E. of Tuamotu Archipelago 53b
Pittsburgh, city, Pennsylvania 26b
Plymouth, port, Devon, England 60c
Poland, rep., central Europe; cap. Warsaw 79b
Popocatepetl ("smoking mountain"), Mexico, S.E. of
    Mexico, height 17,887 ft. 44d
Port-au-Prince, cap. and chief port, Haiti 45c
Port Elizabeth, port, on Algoa B., Cape Prov. 118d
Portland, city, Oregon, on Williamette river 38c
Port Louis, town and cap. of Mauritius 3c
Port of Spain, cap. of Trinidad, W. Indies 45b
Porto Novo, cap. of Dahomey, W. Africa 116a

Portsmouth, city, port and naval base, Hants, England 61c
Portsmouth, town, Virginia 29b
Portugal, republic, S.W. Europe, cap. Lisbon 74c
Portuguese Guinea, colony, W. Africa; cap. Bissau 115c
Prague (Praha), city, Bohemia, cap. of Czechoslovakia 80b
Preston, co. town, Lancs, England, N.E. of Liverpool 59d
Pretoria, city and cap. of S. Africa 118d
Prince Edward Island, prov., Canada; cap. Charlottetown 19d
Principe, Portuguese island, in G. of Guinea, W. Africa 116c
Providence, city & cap. of Rhode I., U.S.A. 25a
Puerto Rico, isl., Greater Antilles, W. Indies 45a
Punjab, state, N.W. India 102b
Pusan, port, S. Korea 95b
Pyongyang, city and cap. of N. Korea 95b
Qatar, sheikdom, Arabia, in The Gulf 107
Quebec, city and cap. of Quebec prov., Canada 18a
Quebec, prov., Canada 13d
Queensland, state, Australia; cap. Brisbane 122d
Quezon City, cap. of the Philippines 99c
Quito, city, cap. of Ecuador, S. America 49a
R.S.F.S.R. = Russian Soviet Federated Socialist Republic
    92 & 93
Rabat, tn. & cap. of Morocco, S W. of Tangier 114c
Rajasthan, state, N.W. India; cap. Jaipur 102b
Rangoon, city and port; cap. of Burma 105c
Rawalpindi, dist. and town, Pakistan 102b
Reading, co. town, Berkshire, England 61c
Recife, city, Brazil, N.E. Brazil 51b
Regina, cap. of Saskatchewan, W. of Winnipeg 15d
Réunion, I., Indian Ocean 3c
Reykjavik, cap. of Iceland, on S.W. coast 56a
Rhode Island, New England state, U.S.A.; cap.
    Providence 25a

St Kitts, island, Leeward Is., W. Indies 45a
St Lawrence, great riv. of N. America; 2340 m. 13d
St Louis, city, Missouri, on the Mississippi 34b
St Lucia, island, Windward group, W. Indies 45b
St Paul, city, Minnesota, on Mississippi 32a
St Petersburg, town, Florida 29d
St Pierre, island, Atlantic, S. of Newfoundland 19b
St Vincent, island, Windward Is., W. Indies 45b
Salford, town, Greater Manchester, England 59b
Salisbury, cap. of Rhodesia, central Africa 119a
Salt Lake City, cap. of Utah, on River Jordan 38b
Salvador, El, rep., Cent. Amer.; cap. San Salvador 44b
San'a, cap. of Yemen, Arabia 106d
San Antonio, city, Texas, W. of Houston 31d
San Diego, city and naval base, California 39d
San Francisco, city and port, California 40d
San José, city and cap. of Costa Rica 44b
San José, town, California 39c
San Juan, cap. of Puerto Rico, W. Indies 45a
San Marino, rep., N.E. Italy 82b
San Salvador, cap. of El Salvador, Cent. America 44b
Santa Ana, town, California 41b
Santa Caterina, state, Brazil 51c
Santiago, city, cap. of Chile, S. America 52a
Santo Domingo, town and cap. of Dominican Rep.,
    West Indies 45a
São Francisco, river, Brazil 51b
São Paulo, city, Brazil, N.W. of Santos 51c
São Paulo, state, Brazil 51c
São Tomé, island in G. of Guinea, W. Africa 116c
Saratov, town, U.S.S.R., S.E. of Moscow 87a
Sarawak, state, E. Malaysia 99d
Saskatchewan, W. prov. of Canada; cap. Regina 12d

Saskatoon, town, Saskatchewan, N.W. of Regina 14b
Saudi Arabia, kingdom, S.W. Asia; cap. Riyadh 106d
Savannah, port, Georgia, U.S.A. 29c
Scotland, northern part of Great Britain; kingdom, cap.
   Edinburgh 62 & 63
Scranton, city, Pennsyl., N.W. of Philadelphia 25c
Seattle, port, Washington, on Puget Sound 41d
Senegal, republic and river, N.W. Africa; cap. Dakar 115c
Seoul (Kyongsong), city and cap. of S. Korea 95b
Sergipe, state, Brazil 51b
Seychelles, Is., Indian Ocean 3c
Shanghai, port, Kiangsu prov., China 97a
Shansi, prov., China 95a
Shantung, prov., China 95c
Sheffield, city, S. Yorks, England 59b
Shensi, prov., China 97c
Shen-yang (Mukden), city, N.E. China 95a
Shreveport, town, Louisiana, U.S.A. 36b
Sian (Changan), cap. of Shensi prov., China 97c
Sierra Leone, rep., W. Africa; cap. Freetown 115d
Sikkim, state, N.E. India; cap. Gangtok 103a
Singapore, island, rep., port and naval base, S. of Malaya 100d
Sinkiang-Uighur, aut. reg., W. China; cap. Urumchi 94a
Slave Lake, Great, N.W. Territories, Canada 12b
Sofia, city, cap. of Bulgaria 83a
Solihull, town, Warwicks., England 60b
Solomon Islands, Melanesia, Pacific Ocean 125d
Somali Republic, state, E. Africa; cap. Mogadishu 117d
Southampton, port, Hampshire, England 61c
South Africa, rep., cap. Pretoria 111b
South Australia, state, Aust.; cap. Adelaide 120d
South Bend, city, Indiana, E. of Chicago 33d
South Carolina, state, U.S.A.; cap. Columbia 29a

South Dakota, state, U.S.A.; cap. Pierre 30c
Southend-on-Sea, seaside resort, Essex, England 61d
South Shields, Tyne & Wear port, Durham, England 59a
South West Africa (Namibia), state, S. Africa 118c
Spain, state, S.W. Europe; cap. Madrid 74b
Spanish Sahara, prov., W. Africa 114d
Spitsbergen, islands, Arctic Oc., N. of Norway 3a
Spokane, town, Washington, N.E. of Portland 38c
Springfield, town, Massachusetts, S.W. of Boston 24b
Sri Lanka (Ceylon), rep., I. off S. India; cap. Colombo 101
Stanley, port and cap. of Falkland Is. 52d
Stewart Island, to south of South I., N.Z. 127c
Stockholm, port and cap. of Sweden 67a
Stockport, town, Cheshire, England 60b
Stoke-on-Trent, city, Staffs, England 60b
Stuttgart, city, W. Germany 78c
Sucre, town and cap. of Bolivia 50c
Sudan, rep., N.E. Africa; cap. Khartoum 117a
Sudbury, town, Ontario, N.W. of Montreal 15b
Sunderland, port, Tyne & Wear, England 59a
Superior, L., Canada and U.S.A.; length 360 m. 13c
Surabaja, port, Java, Indonesia 99d
Surinam, prov. of Netherlands, S. America 48a
Svalbard, arch., Arctic Ocean 66c & 10a
Sverdlovsk, town in Ural Mts, U.S.S.R. 90c
Swansea, port, W. Glamorgan, Wales 60c
Swaziland, kingdom, S. Africa 119c
Sweden, kingdom, Scandinavia, W. Europe; cap
    Stockholm 67a
Switzerland, rep., central Europe, cap. Berne 76c
Sydney, city, cap. of New South Wales 123b
Syracuse, town, New York, E. of Rochester 24d
Syria, rep., W. Asia; cap. Damascus 106a

Tōkyō, city and cap. of Japan, Honshu I. 96a
Toledo, town, Ohio, W. of Cleveland 26d
Tolima, mt., Colombia 48c
Tonga Islands, Polynesia, Pacific Ocean 53d
Topeka, city, cap. of Kansas, U.S.A. 30b
Torbay, town, Devon, England 60d
Toronto, city, cap. of Ontario, Canada 17c
Torrance, town, California 41b
Transvaal, prov., S. Africa; cap. Pretoria 118d
Trenton, city and cap. of New Jersey 25c
Trinidad, island, W. Indies, part of rep. of Trinidad and
    Tobago; cap. Port of Spain 48a
Tripoli, port and naval base, Libya 112c
Tristan da Cunha, volcanic island, S. Atlantic Oc. 111d
Tsingtao (Ch'ing-tao), port, Shantung, on Kiaochow Bay 95c
Tucson, town, Arizona, S.E. of Phoenix 39b
Tulsa, town, Oklahoma 31a
Tunis, town and cap. of Tunisia 114a
Tunisia, rep., North Africa; cap. Tunis 114a
Tupungato, mt., S. America 52a
Turin, town, Piedmont, N. Italy 84d
Turkey, rep., Europe and Asia; cap. Ankara 108c
Turkmenistan, rep., U.S.S.R.; cap. Ashkhabad 90d
Turks Islands, group of islands, S. of the Bahamas 45a
U.A.R. (Egypt) now Arab Republic of Egypt 112b
U.K. = United Kingdom of Great Britain and Northern
    Ireland 58
U.S.A. = United States of America 20 & 21
U.S.S.R. = Union of Soviet Socialist Republics 92 & 93
Ufa, town, U.S.S.R., S.W. of Sverdlovsk 87a
Uganda, state, Africa; cap. Entebbe 117c
Ukraine, rep., U.S.S.R.; cap. Kiev (Kiyev) 88c
Ulaanbaatar, town and cap. of Mongolia 94b

Union of Soviet Socialist Republics, state, Europe and
  Asia; cap. Moscow 92 & 93
United Kingdom of Great Britain and Northern Ireland,
  state, W. Europe; cap. London 58
United States of America, state, N. America; cap.
  Washington 20 & 21
Upper Volta, rep., W. Africa; cap. Ouagadougou 115a
Uruguay, rep. and river, S. America; length 950 m.
  cap. Montevideo 47a
Utah, inland state, U.S.A.; cap. Salt Lake City 38b
Uttar Pradesh, state, India; chief tn. Lucknow 104d
Utica, town, New York, N.W. of Albany 24d
Uzbekistan, rep., U.S.S.R.; cap. Tashkent 90d
Vaduz, cap. of principality of Liechtenstein 76a
Valencia, port, Spain, on east coast 75c
Valletta, port and cap. of Malta 82d
Vancouver, city & port, Brit. Columbia, W. Canada, N. of
  Victoria 14d
Vänern, lake, S.W. Sweden; length 95 m. 67c
Venezuela, rep., S. America; cap. Caracas 48c
Vermont, a New England state, U.S.A.; cap. Montpelier
  24a
Vesuvius, Mount, vol., Italy, on B. of Naples 82d
Victoria, state, S.E. Aust.; cap. Melbourne 123b
Victoria, cap. of Br. Columbia, on Vancouver I. 14d
Victoria, cap. and chief port, Hong Kong 95c
Victoria, Lake, Africa, between Uganda, Tanzania and
  Kenya 117c
Vienna (Wien), city, cap. of Austria, on Danube 80b
Vientiane, town and cap. of Laos, on Mekong R. 98b
Vietnam, N. and S., reps., S.E. Asia 98b
Virgin Islands, group in West Indies 45a
Virginia, a S. Atlantic state, U.S.A.; cap. Richmond 22b